Pre-Apocalyptic
The SkullFuck Collection

Jeremy Void

Other books by Jeremy Void

Derelict America

Nefarious Endeavors

Smash a Lightbulb:
Poetry for Lowlifes

Erase Your Face:
The SkullFuck Collection

Just a Kid

Sex Drugs & Violence:
Incomplete Stories for the Incomplete Human

An Art Form:
The Crass Poetry Collection

My Story:
The Short Version

I Need Help:
The SkullFuck Collection

The Lost Letters

Chaos Writing

*The TR*TH*

My Psychedelic Suicide

A Crass Philosophy:
The SkullFuck Collection

Postal Prose

Spoken word albums by Jeremy Void

Absurd Nihilism

Word Vomit

Pre-Apocalyptic: The SkullFuck Collection

Copyright © 2016 by Jeremy Void

All Rights Reserved

No part of this book may be reproduced, scanned, or distributed in any print or electronic form without permission. Please do not participate in or encourage piracy of copyrighted materials in violation of the author's rights. Purchase only authorized editions.

ISBN Number:
978-0-578-18833-1

ChaosWriting **Press**

It's a Mindfuck
www.chaoswriting.net

To All My Friends
all those who've made this possible
To The Rutland Punks And Metalheads
the runts and the rebels
To Everyone Else Who Helped Me Along My Way

THIS ONE'S FOR YOU

🌐 Intro

Jeremy Void is the author of 11 books.

- 💼 **Author at** Chaos Writing
- 🎓 **Studied Head splitting at** The American Institute Of 'Beat My Head'
- 🎓 **Studied Lewd sexual remarks at** Insensitivity Tech
- 🎓 **Studied Booze & pills at** University of Nowhere
- 🎓 **Goes to** The Homicidal Zoo
- 🏠 **Lives in** Rutland , Vermont
- 📍 **From** Boston, Massachusetts
- 📡 **Followed by** 19 people

the bloody, gooey guts & organs & winding intestines that spiderweb through the insides of this book, winding and spinning a delicate system of inners that spill off the page and lurch straight outward and wind their distorted, blurry, and every so fucked-up way around your disjointed head, your crooked neck, your lopsided shoulders, and hold you there in their terroristic vice-like grasp—just holding you steady, keeping you there neat and ordered and rotten and ugly like the fat pig that you are—as the mammoth shaft rises from deep down within, springing upward like a psychotic, murderous jack-in-the-box, and zeroes in on one of your eyeballs, locks you in its sights like a heat-seeking missile on a seek-&-fuck senseless mission, a find-&-dominate assignment which your teacher wielding a long, black leather whip had assigned the day before with a snap and crackle of said whip (yeah, that kind of mission), and then proceeds to cockthrust your eyesocket again and again and again until you start to enjoy it, and you will enjoy it, guaranteed:

I'm 29 today and I swear in a year I'll go out like Hunter S. Thompson, or at least that WAS the plan, but I slashed out my 30-year-old suicide pact when I became old enough to grasp that I got at least another 40 years to go and millions of more roads to explore and hundreds of more people to annoy, more buttons to find, more levers to crank, more words to abuse, more truths to disuse; so I'm 29-years old, and I think I've got some more living to do….

Jeremy Void
July 30 at 5:02pm

Wake me up when I'm famous.

👍 Like   💬 Comment   ➤ Share

IT IS ONLY SELF-EXPRESSION DON'T TAKE IT SO LITERALLY

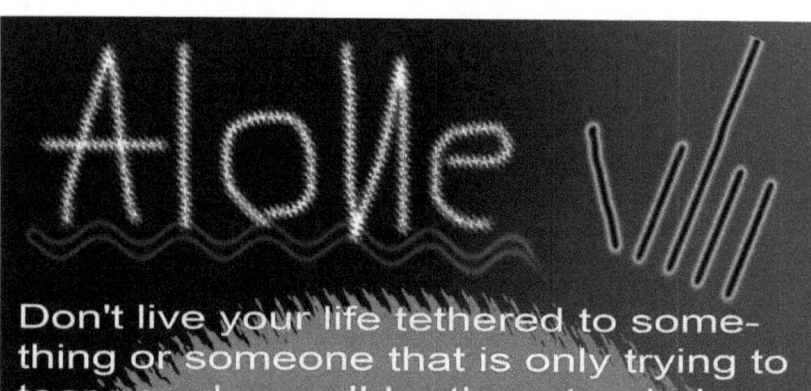

Alone

Don't live your life tethered to something or someone that is only trying to tear you down. I'd rather stand alone than be attached at the hip to a nefarious beast. Love and lust, two things that I could do without, two things I mix up way too often, two things that always tear me down. Don't live your life attached to nothing, live free and wild, but don't mistake love for a flame because you'll come to find out that it's really a vicious snake trying to bite your head off. Freedom is lonely but loving someone kills....

day in day out

day in day out we
kicked life in the balls
spat in its face—
day in day out.

we rode the bull till the bull
bit dirt, then we dismounted
& kicked it in the head
punched it in the face until
blood spurted & pooled beneath
its head.

on the subway, in back alleys, atop
bridges & underneath the railroad tracks
we ran & frolicked in our own filth,
creating more filth for the yuppie class to
clean up. we did all, knocking back &
cracking skulls, hopping pogoing flailing
& divebombing till the last mans dead.

life is a beast, a great big fuckin beast
that we maimed w/ a two-by-four, speared it
w/ our own fists, & pelted it w/
our steel-toed boots. blood splattering in
our toothless faces—& we smiled amid
the gore. our grins sick & freakish,
wide & missing teeth.

like bonnie & clyde, we robbed the yuppies
blind, big businesses cringed at all the mischief
we stirred, the hell we conjured up & blasted
in their faces.

thats right, you & me babe, we
delivered fierce stabs, stabbing the outsiders
in their backs, necks, & faces, piercing their hearts
w/ our own spiked tongues.

we did it all, day in day out,
& then we went home

& went to bed.

Before AA I was lying on my couch listening to a CD I made—999, the Clash, the Adverts, Cock Sparrer, the Adicts—and I was thinking, *I still like Punk rock, definitely like it, maybe even love it*—no, just like it—*but I can't relate to it as much because I'm not a teenager anymore, however still bored, frustrated, not AS angry, immature, a little wild*—not like I was—*and crazy, but the music doesn't speak to me like it used to;* so I threw my Monster at the wall, making things right: Punk rock.

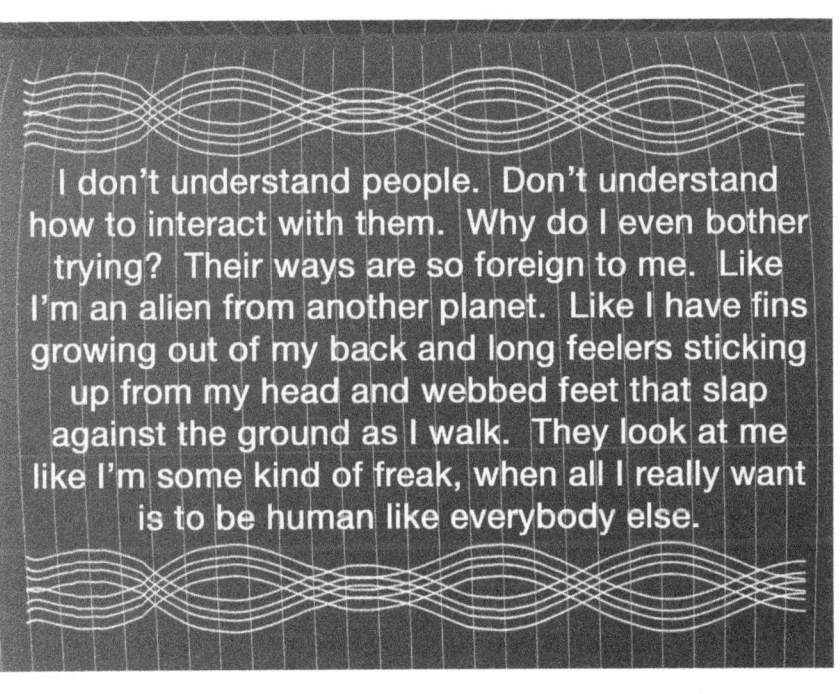

I don't understand people. Don't understand how to interact with them. Why do I even bother trying? Their ways are so foreign to me. Like I'm an alien from another planet. Like I have fins growing out of my back and long feelers sticking up from my head and webbed feet that slap against the ground as I walk. They look at me like I'm some kind of freak, when all I really want is to be human like everybody else.

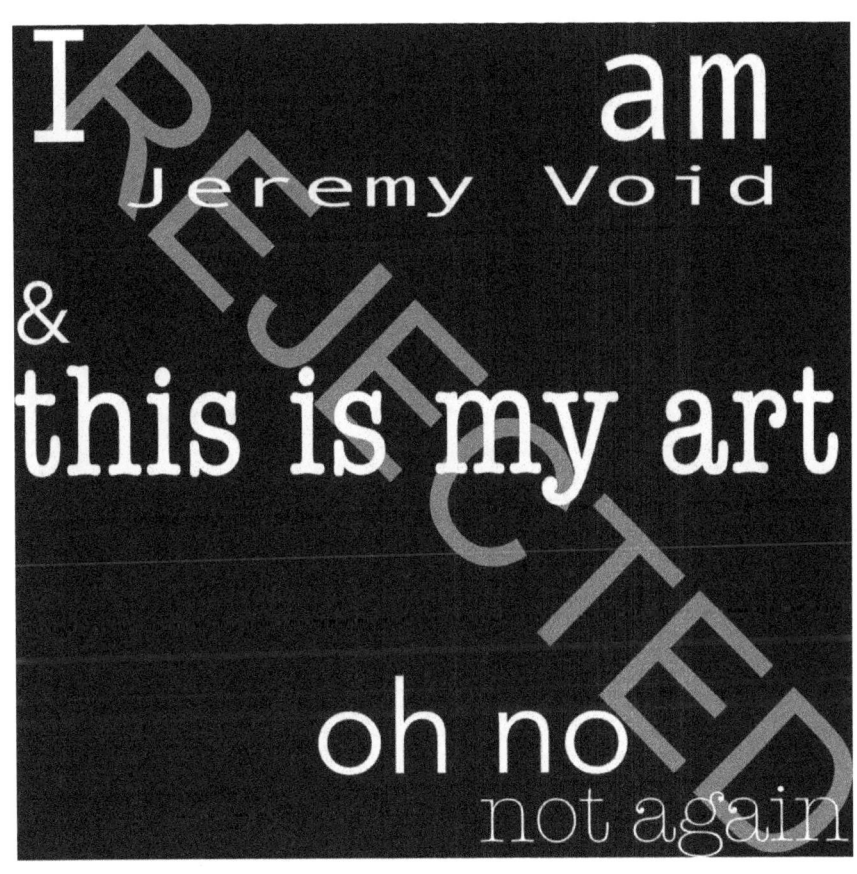

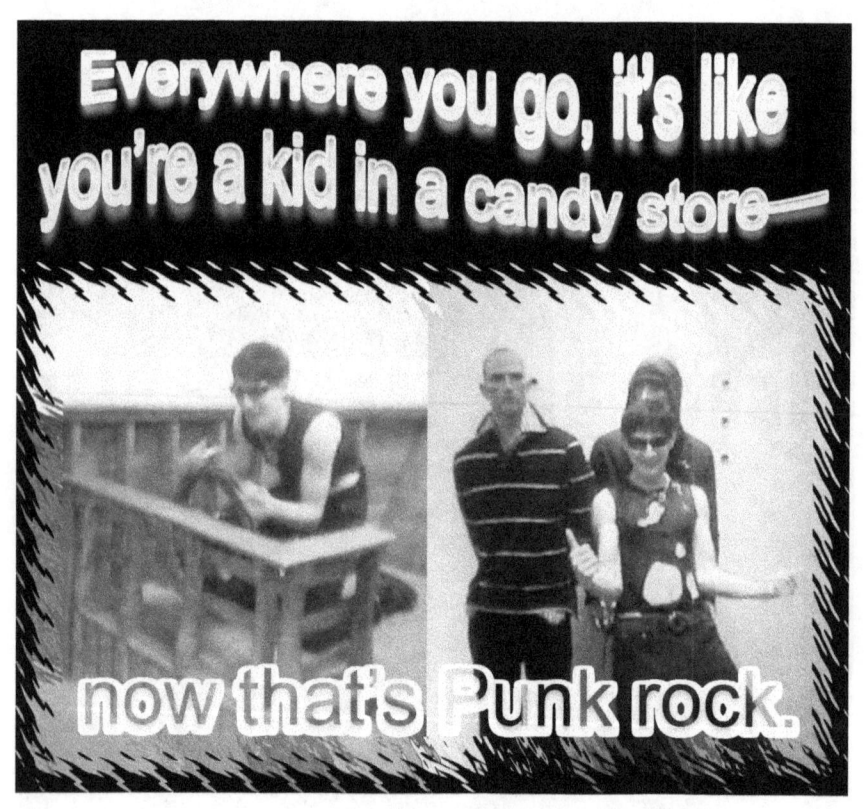

Point & Click

Burn Out

I can't find the right words to say what I'm feeling. Usually I'm on a roll, but today self-doubt has taken its toll. I hate my face, the way it smirks when I'm all alone, sneers and growls and I feel oh so cold. I get energetic and wild and I do what I please. I get frenetic and shy and I can't do anything. Boxed in—intense energy holding me stiff, too much of it makes me hate existence. I burn out from time to time, I'm only human. It's times like these when I just wanna die. This past week I wrote almost twelve pieces, two are stories and ten are poems. But it's all garbage, I know now; I'll pile it up and douse it with gas, light a match and let the flame do the rest. I'm sorry if we ever spoke, I'm sorry I got to know you. I'm losing a dream of the past that's gotten too mean, and now I'm suffering and slipping and sinking into a pit that's way too deep. Do I care only so others will care, or do I care simply because I'm a caring person. It's pointless anyway, throw caution to the wind; your right and wrong just don't seem to fit for a person like me.

↑evolution

im slowly learning the ways
of the world, like i was born jus yesterday
& growing older at a rapid rate.
every event, every moment, every
failed effort, every successful endeavor—
it all adds up until one day
soon i hope
i gain control of my own fate
& i no longer haveta rely on others
to take me there. but on my own accord
i can rise above the ranks & be so much
better than the man i was the day before.

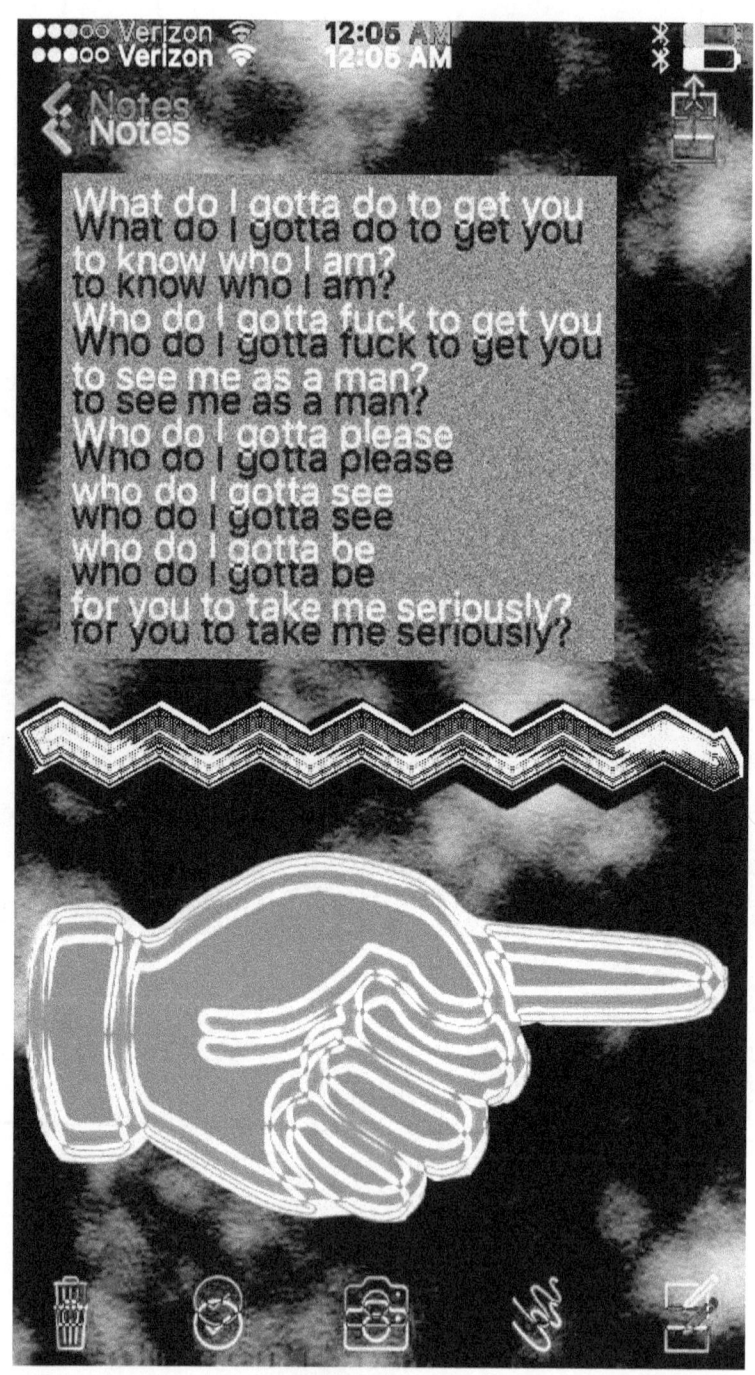

Before I go on I must say I'm not really such a miserable person after all, as my written voice might portray me as. No, I'm usually quite pleasant but at times I'm not so pleasant and I do my best writing in these states—so, there!

I feel like complete fucking shit today. **NOW** how do I exploit that feeling??

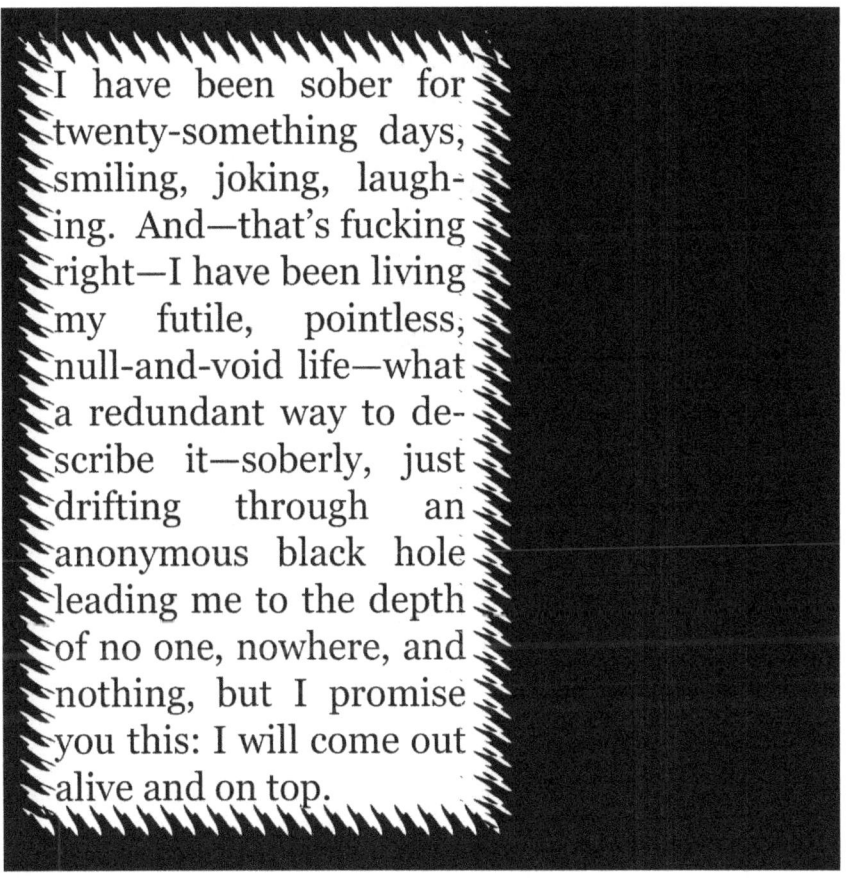

I have been sober for twenty-something days, smiling, joking, laughing. And—that's fucking right—I have been living my futile, pointless, null-and-void life—what a redundant way to describe it—soberly, just drifting through an anonymous black hole leading me to the depth of no one, nowhere, and nothing, but I promise you this: I will come out alive and on top.

Sorry I don't paint the walls blue with hope,
but splatter bloody bricks through the windows of destructive art.

Sorry I don't make you feel good, like everything is oh so wonderful in life and it's never been better and I'm pushing and pushing through the helpless swamps on my way to be great,
but instead set the swamps on fire and run through the flames naked as Twin Towers everywhere collapse in spurts of smoke and steam and this–this–THIS–is my reason to live.

Sorry I'm not ten-feet tall with a gut full of food and a mind that ruminates relentlessly about the needs of others, and and and–you know–
because I'm selfish and stubborn and yet I'm doing my best to help out others who come my way; but even so your existence doesn't usually cross my mind unless you're right there in front of me.

Sorry my poetry doesn't spin webs of phony prayers of hope and fabricated wonder that brings you joyful tears, but instead
it's like a submachine gun as the bullets tear into a condemned man and he's screaming and crying as I pull the trigger....

Trust me, I am good and I'm doing the best I can, and I'm getting better every day I set down one foot after another, and I'm plowing my own way through a shit-filled existence with liars who will cut you down before you step one foot out your door, and I'm living honestly and I give and I give, although you wouldn't know anything about it because I don't vocalize my acts of goodness–wait, I just did.

In short: Sorry I'm not a liar.

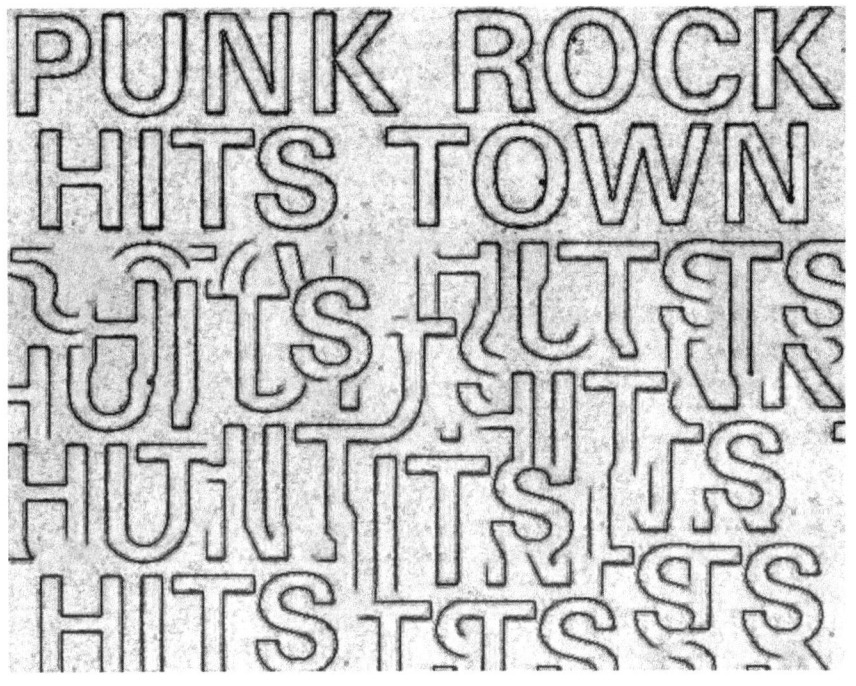

I am not like ordinary men. I think in a way that makes the mass populous shudder. My thoughts and dreams are banned from most libraries, my ideas and schemes forbidden from any textbook. I'm just a human being trying to navigate my way through a world crammed tight with let-downs and set-backs. I write because I need to, not because I want to, but there's a magic beneath the pen as it scrawls word for word, as I scribble my internal drama between the lines. It's almost like giving birth, painful to let it out, but boy does it feel good that it will fester inside you no longer, and now you can raise and nourish it.
That's a magical thing, isn't it?

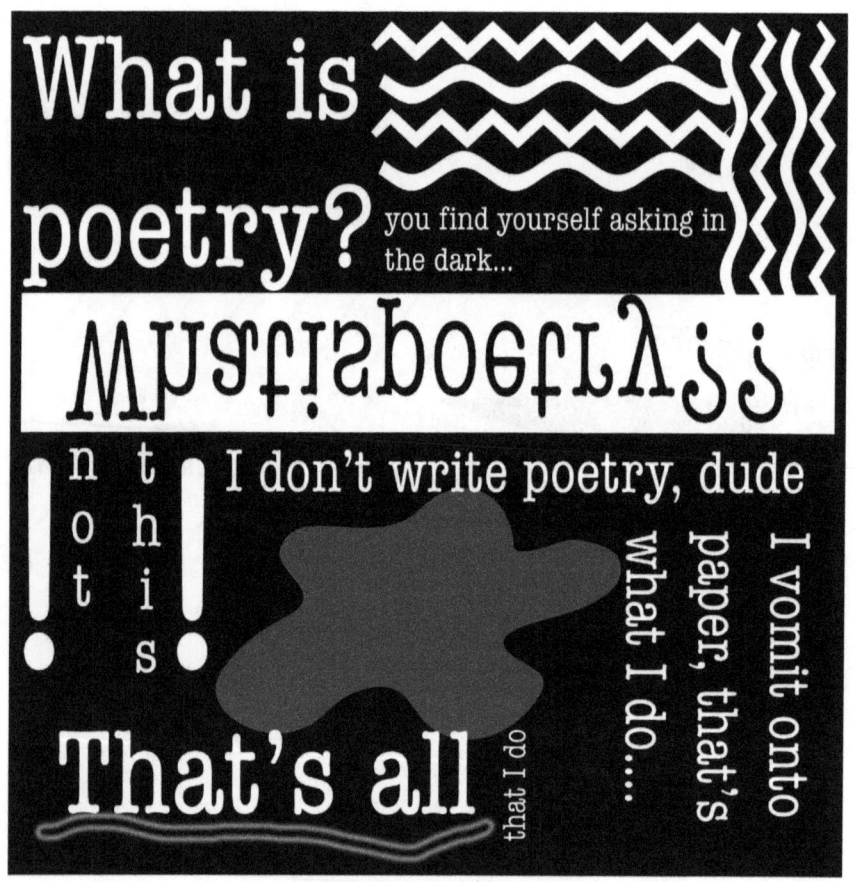

Punk Rock Song

We stalk the streets in tattered wear.
We sit on rooftops without a care.
Drinking forties and liquor galore,
we sing our songs and scream fuck the world.

We band together in ghoulish suits.
We fight together with fists and boots.
The streets aren't safe, we know this well.
But we stay as one, and as one we'll yell.

I'm think I'm gonna make myself manic
I mean really **MANIC**
Like off the wall
Cuz I'm curious about something.
Besides I'm happier when I'm manic.
so it begins

I love words; I love everything about them—the way they make me feel, the way they make me think. Words are my ecstasy. They flow through me like gas, they make me cum a thousand colors—colors actual and abstract. I love words; love to mold and manipulate them into vivid depictions so visceral I shudder with each syllable, each sound that comes out. I paint with words, I write people and images and creations so magnificent I feel complete and significant. They lift me up and knock me down and spin me round and round, a rollercoaster of alliteration and rhymes—a thrilling downward spiral that twists and loops around and shoots up, before the sudden crashing plunge. So hysterical I am about words that I want the whole world to know. I wanna stand on the edge of tall buildings, the whirring wind buzzing, my clothes fluttering. I'll cup my hands around my mouth and scream—I LOVE WORDS!!!

Most alcoholics/drug addicts live on the edge. My problem was that I didn't have an edge to live on, cuz I'd fallen off it at a very early age. I spent the greater part of my life falling. Falling to my bottom. I kicked and flailed, trying to grab hold of something, but there was nothing I couldn't break.... Everything that came my way and I managed to sink my teeth into snapped like a twig beneath the weight of my plunge. It was hopeless!

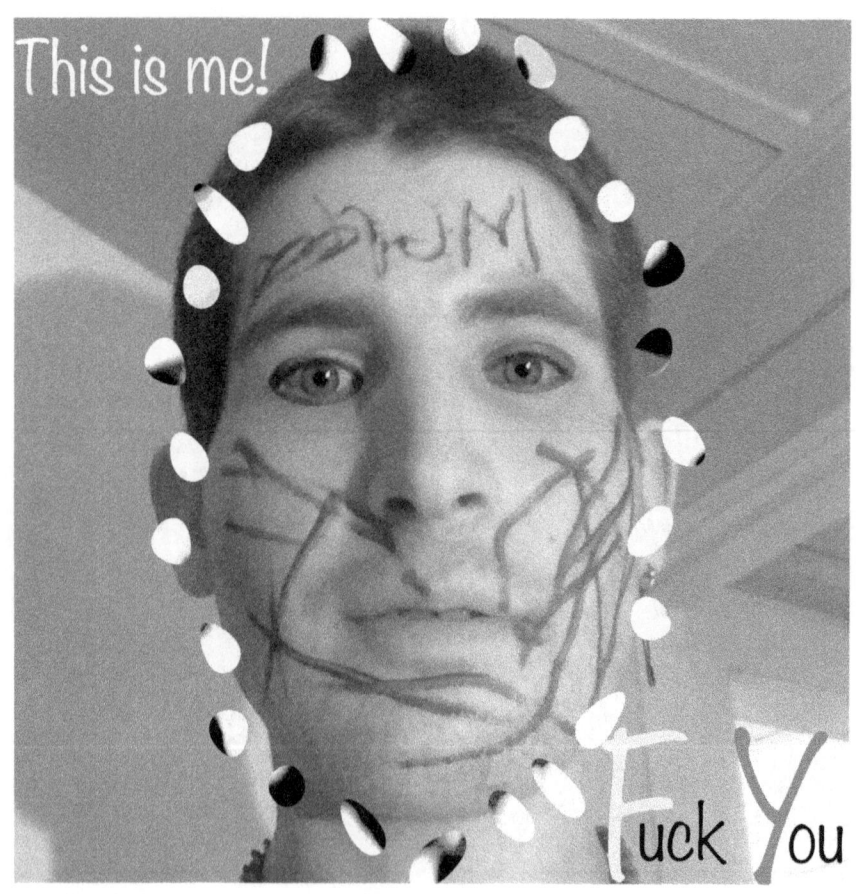

MY ARCH NEMESIS

The thing I hate most about you
is
the fact
that I see me when I look into
your filthy fucking eyes.

I Am What I Am

Know what pisses me off? Aside from everything. It's when I post something positive and it picks up so much more LIKEs than my darker stuff. I know people want me to do well, want me to be happy (although, to tell you the truth, it would make me very happy if people LIKEd my darker stuff as well as my positive stuff because then I would know that it's being received, but no, nobody cares about making me happy). No wonder people live fake lives on Facebook, pretending to be happy. It's like when I worked at Panera Bread and my managers would urge me to smile even though I was not happy. No one cares if I'm happy, they just want me to pretend so that THEY can feel good. Well, fuck you all, this is who I am!

& I'll Do What I Do

Life is good

I don't have enough good friends around here. Most my friends learn to hate me eventually cuz they can't take the insanity. Two weeks ago I spent all night with this chick and I told her in exactly a week from tonight you will hate me. She said she wouldn't. She promised me she wouldn't. She hasn't returned any of my Facebook message in the past week. Started on Friday when she stopped responding to me, exactly a week after I made the statement that she will hate me in exactly a week. What a fucking a hypocrite! But everyone's a poser, when you think about it. No one knows who they are and what they're doing in this place. We're all lost souls wandering the earth purposelessly, searching for answers, reasons, but around every turn is a wall and we find that we're really boxed in, just walking in circles inside our box. Whatever that means. Life is good. Aside from making some new enemies last week, life is awesome. I smoked weed the other night, which sucks. a bit of a setback, cuz it'd been almost 2 years since I'd gotten high. But it's not the end of the world.

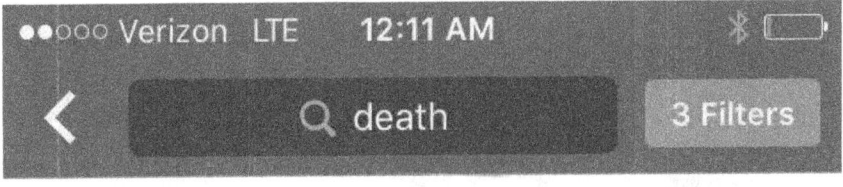

In the car with ▓▓▓ coming back from the show in Rhode Island, gonna crash at his pad for the night because by the time we reach Quincy MA the train will have stopped running, in fact they already have. Because it is in fact 2 AM and they would have stopped at about 12:30 AM, roughly, and we're cruising down the highway, got the Lower Class Brats playing on the stereo, and everything is cool, no worries, no cares in world because life is good like how it should be; I'm heading back to Vermont on Cape Air tomorrow afternoon—fun fun fun!

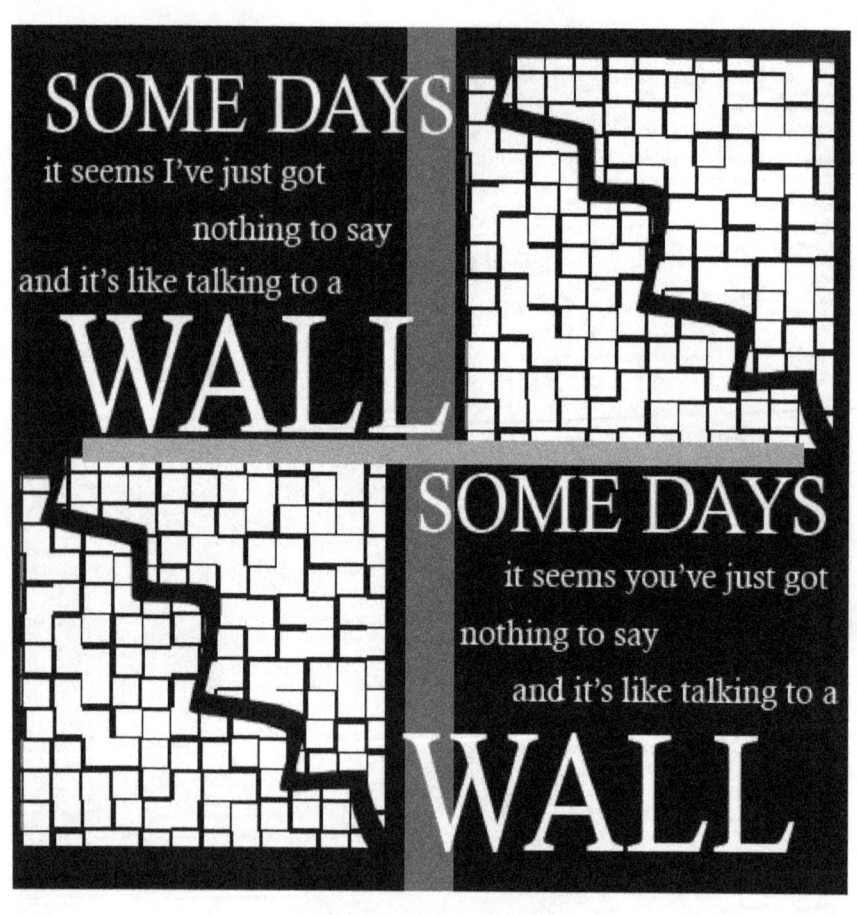

I want everyone to read
this poem.
I'll shove it in your face
if I haveta.

Better yet, I don't want
you to read it.
Because maybe then
you'll sully it with your
ugliness.

Two weeks ago I had a crappy week (although of course there were the good parts too, or else the shit-storm explosive manic fucked-up reactive fatalistic behaviors I exhibited by the end of it all wouldn't have happened, and the week would have resulted in an entirely different outcome). But I have to say I learned a lot from it all and I believe I came out a better person. Sometimes one has to lose their mind to gain a greater understanding which would not have been achieved if one's mind stayed in place, sedated and relentlessly humdrum. I'm not excusing the way I acted, because I was a complete and total dick to everyone who came my way, but I'm just saying that sometimes things get way too tame and complacent and the only way to make any further forward motion is to stir the melting pot round and round and round until it erupts like a volcano, and the fact that I came out the other side with some people gunning after me is only an unfortunate consequence to gaining wisdom. If you've never experienced any form of hysteria, wasting away behind a desk locked inside a cubicle just waiting to die as you pound out red tape after red tape imagining what the barrel of the gun must taste like before you pull the trigger—if that's you, then I don't expect you to understand. Yesterday when I told someone what had happened, read the story I wrote to depict my week at my Creative Writing group on Fridays, one woman said she thought I was making growth but then this happened and now she doesn't know. But I am making growth; just sometimes things must

EXPLODE...

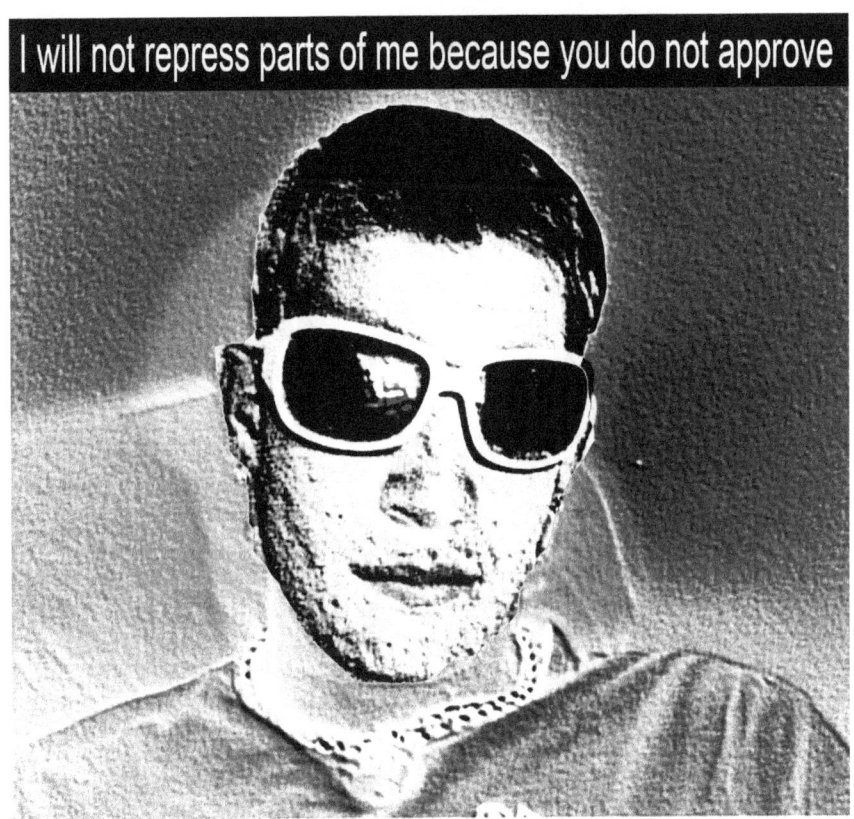

Point & Click

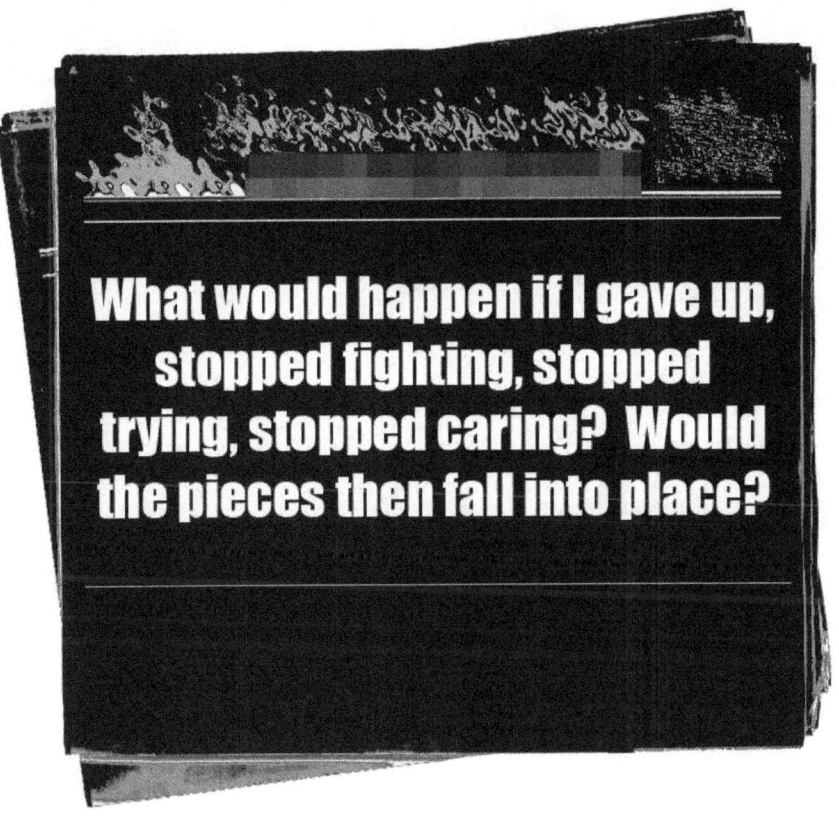

What would happen if I gave up, stopped fighting, stopped trying, stopped caring? Would the pieces then fall into place?

DEATH TO FASCIST
PUNKS

I joined this group on Facebook called "Punk Rock Community" cuz I thought it would be a great place to showcase my Punk rock poetry, as after all I am a Punk rock poet.

But they all had only one thing on their minds: CENSORSHIP

Another Kind of Pretty

My hair is charged.
My sunglasses shine.
My mind is sharp.
I'm looking so fine.

I stagger
I swagger.
My body sways
as I walk down the street.

I see her there, she looks so neat.
Her colored hair, her torn T-shirt.
Her tight leather and a slew of piercings
that make my heart stop beating.

I don't know if she can see me.
She's another kind of pretty.
I hope she can see me,
cuz I'm another kind of something.

darkness

another cigarette smoked.
another cup of coffee drunk.
i sit in the dark as my mind
races like a racecar dashing
my hands trembling faster.
the coffee cup jingles in my
jittery hands.
another day spent.
another day lost.
a maddening worry erupting inside
me like a racking pain thrumming deep
deep
deep
deep in my sub-conscious.
the tv showing static.
the sound buzzing like a
pack of bumble bees.
i hate the sound but i
let it play regardless because
its much better than that....

that which will kill me.

killing the silence

**I CANT STAND silence.
i fill the gaps w/ VIOLENCE—**

senseless acts to fill the gaps
that make me mad w/ rage.
i hate the nothingness that
roils when nothing is going down.
im bleeding cant you see
my heart gushing thick red streams.
i bleed because theres not a thing
to do in this boring old town.
its a rut i tell you, a fuckin rut
that bores me to fuckin death.
the only thing left for me to do
is beat my head against this red brick wall.
ill beat it till i fall.

I Am Stuck.
I Am Scared
I Am Lost
I Don't Know Where I Am Going
I Don't Know What I Am
I Should Just Kill Myself
I'm Afraid of Everything
and Everyone
Bite the Bullet Is the Only Valid Solution
I Never Should Have Lived This Long Anyway
The World Is Shit
Everyone Pretending to Be Happy
All Smiles
Misery
Hate
My Fate Is Dissolving
I'm Melting into Ashes
This Is Definitely a Cry for Help
But Please Ignore Me

Lies   Lies
everything's a lie

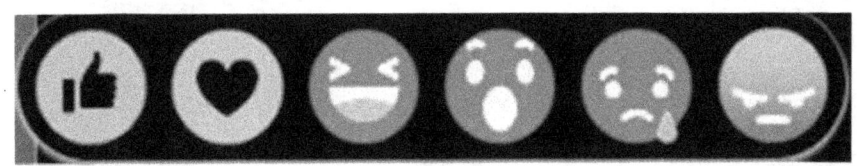

Life is great, and to all those who think otherwise, which I'm sure there are a lot of you out there, open up your fucking eyes and look around you, and quit your boring ass brooding; it's getting old. Life is good, so you can all go suck a cock!

The World Was Mine
but I stomped on its head

If I told you how I truly felt, well you know how that goes: Now this person hates me. If I told you the truth skewed by own beliefs, well you know how that goes: I lose another friend. If I spelled it out to you in blood and guts and fed it to you on a silver platter, well you know how that goes: I'd have nobody left. In the end all I've got is me, becuz the world hates this man I've become. The world hates the man I can be. The world hates when I live truthfully. I believe that art is the truth, I believe that true art holds no bounds, I believe a lot of things, but when I live true to those beliefs, well you know how that goes: I end up all alone. I'm a sadist. I use self-expression as a way to channel my hateful ways. But in the end it all boils down to one last thing, living in an existence ridden with diseased minds and diseased freaks, and I'm the creep? If I told you how I truly felt, well guess what, I must be insane....

Confessions

I'm stuck in a daydream. This is not the way it's supposed to be. Me, alone---no, I like it that way (but, lonely?). Me, disturbed---there ain't no other way. I create turmoil where there isn't, and peace where there is. I'm an addict. Pleasure drives me insane. When I feel GOOD, I think to myself, *If only I had more.* That's my problem, don't you see. Seeking excess, taking all that I can take, and leaving nothing left behind. A week and a half ago I met a girl---spent all morning with her at the coffee shop. The following day walked the streets with her until the morning light infected the world like a virus. Best time I had in a long time, and I didn't want it to end. So I embraced the pleasure and I wouldn't let go. Until she let go for me and I plunged straight into the arms of an old friend of mine---mania.
Now people hate me---but what can I do?

Last night I smoked weed---for those who don't know---haven't gotten high in almost 2 years. The night before I strolled down to the store in search of some kind of chemical euphoria; but I couldn't find what I was looking for. Wanted to do acid---probably good that I didn't---but the blackmarket had run out and all that was left was marijuana.

I know I've been insane---what can I say? I know my moods have been changing, from day to day, hour to hour, minute to minute, and in a heartbeat I might do you in. But please don't hate me for it! Because I'm beating myself up enough as it is and I don't need any more pressure coming down on my head. See, pleasure is the enemy, it's the root of my torment, it's the one thing I can't fight back against; I'm vulnerable and lost.

If I ever experience nirvana, I might very well blow my brains out. Take a knife and carve out my heart and pin it up on the bulletin board. In February an old girlfriend said I'm not the same anymore, I'm not insane like I used to be; all I wanna do is read and write. I told her, to quote one of my favorite poets Richard Hell, "I'd rather write a poem than be a person any day." Because writing poetry is easier than dealing with people, it's easier and safer. And she said I'm asking her to love a poem, and she can't love a poem. So I told her to Fuck Off. I don't need her anyway. But what she'd said stuck in my heart, and when that girl said I lack self-confidence, the time bomb started ticking, a 5-day lifespan. It took 5 days for me to lose control---of my mouth, of my mind. 'Actions speak louder than words.' Last Friday my words were rather loud. I threatened her ex-boyfriend, grabbed my knife, and on my way there I realized what am I going to do once I get there? Yesterday a friend said her ex-boyfriend would have killed me. But maybe that's what I want right now. To die. Maybe that will bring about endless pleasure---a dream come true.

Or endless pain, whatever. To me pleasure and pain result in the same state of consciousness---madness---but nothingness results in boredom and the only way out of that is pleasure or pain and therefore I'm screwed. So what am I to do??

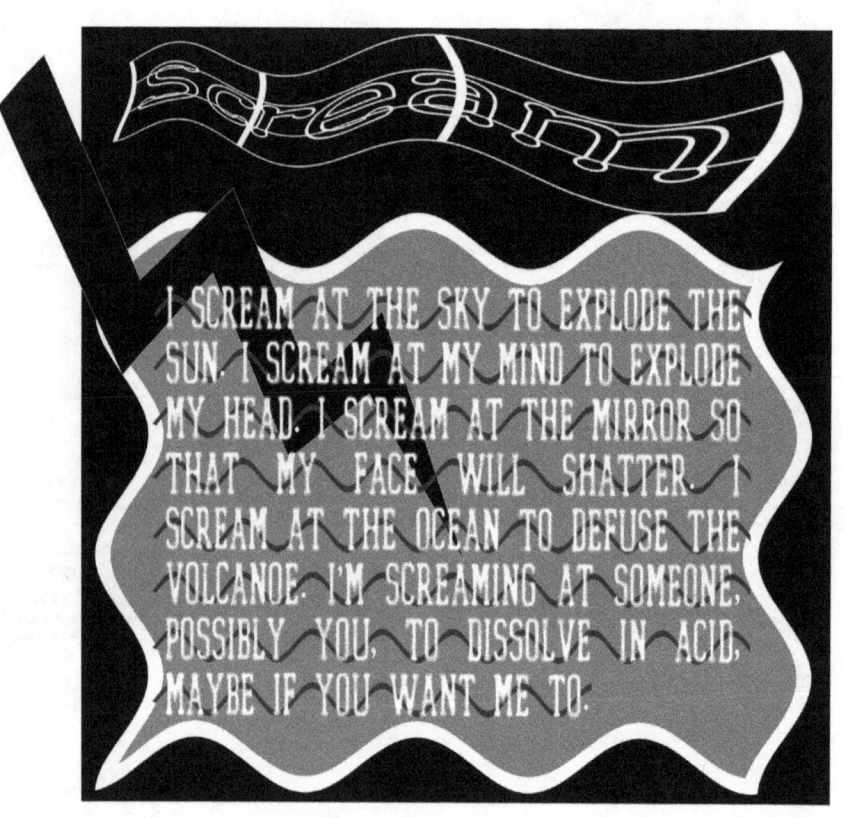

It might not be for everyone

but hopefully it's for someone

Step into My Void, join my hand why won't you?/// I'll show you a world you never knew existed....

I'll tear away your veil, I'll hand you my mask, and together we'll march through the shade of nothingness, going nowhere and expecting less—no hope is all you'll find here, a futureless chaos that will lift you up and make you high... just the two of us.

We'll dance on glass floors that loom high over a bleeding city, a beaten world; we'll boogie as bombs blow holes in the universe—up here it'll be just you and I going closer to my black hole.

A vacuum winding beautiful spirals to paint filthy backdrops that glow vacantly, like a ghostly desert. Walk with me as I show you the pure bliss that My Void has in store. Watch as the world goes to hell around us.

But here in My Void everything will be fine.... Step into My Void and I'll show you something magical—something you could never imagine, not even in your wildest dreams. Babe, it'll be pure emptiness, a jaded wasteland, a lustful sort of nothingness that's so nihilistically sound...

I'll show you the meaning of life/

you'll realize it don't mean shit...

I'll show you the reason to live/

you'll realize it's just a moot point

Step into My Void and you'll never be the same again....

People are all the same. We paint ourselves with words—I do it too. I mean I'm a writer after all. We all have images of who we should be, and we tell others as if that's who we are. But in the end we're no different than anyone else. Sick, fucked-up individuals who want to use, manipulate, and destroy. We hate, we divide, and we conquer. The point of life: power. Finding power, destroying power, taking power. We're all the same, everyone's the same. We hate, we fuck, and we kill. That's the name of the game. I'm a very tolerant person, I tolerate everyone, but fuck you anyway!

...ce I slept, jus...
...orking on work, unneces...
...wrong when the cigarettes you smoke...
...ation thre...ding its way up to the sky hove...
...e an ecstatic blanket, and the dots, they com...
...e your very eyes dancing and zigzagging acros...
...en—your depth perception playing relentless games...
...ur hearing and you can hear the music coming from yo...
alls coming from a bush outside, your cat cries in melod...
...ails that sound an awful lot like the music coming from you...
walls, and the dots did I mention the dots? dancing and scat-
tering across the ceiling and the smoke and the dots and the
voices don't sound like my voice anymore, the pitch fluctuat-
ing in erratic arrays of turbulence and you want your neigh-
bor to turn off the tunes. You recognize the song now. I bang
my fist on the wall and say SHUT IT. The dots and the smok...
...d then I realize I was the source of the smoke, me and th...
...s are still dancing and dancing and dancing and they...
...ble spiders all coming at me, and I scratch the wall.
I scratch my head, I scratch my balls, I scratch my...
...e stands there and stares at me but I'm not real...
...d I be? In purgatory, maybe floating s...
...d there I am typing something about...
...o matter when I'm looking i...

Ive loved and Ive lost
Ive come and Ive gone
Ive been there done that
round and round and round
It's sad isn't it? when the
whole world is obsessed
with LOVE.
DeStRoY WhAt yOu lOvE
before it destroys you....
overdone // overplayed
luv is so cliche.
boring boring boring
I'm sick & I'm bored and I'm
screaming for something more....
Tell Me Something I Don't Know

...uch as I use...
...m, i mean *fantasy*, by the w...
...dream (fantasy) i had—cant remem...
...aybe that means ive lowered my expecta...
...used to be a bit of an idealist, always in an e...
...ed-up nihilism) funk. it really got me down. y...
...d to be a nihilist—only i always pronounced th...
...even tho i *knew* the actual pronunciation (i d...
...cing words properly, id say—pure nihilism...
...pronouncing it this way (niy-ilism) my...
...hange for nobody)—but i cud n...
...beyond the scope of...

So What

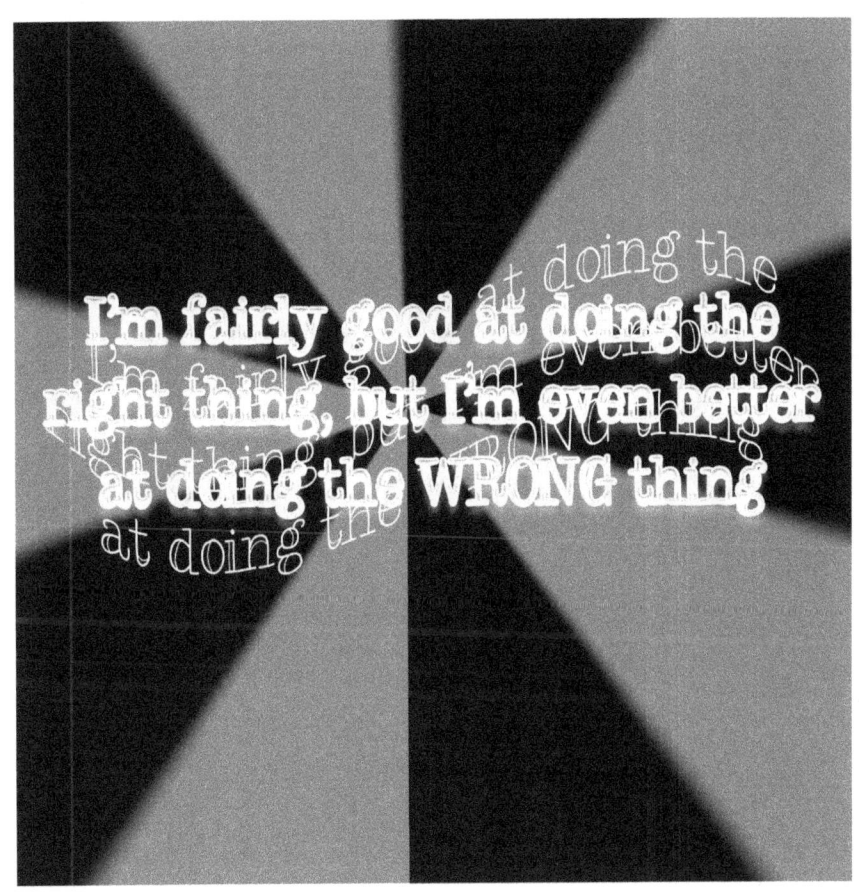

So glad to be in Boston again. The beautiful city shimmers beneath my feet. I laugh amid the cacophony of noise and lights and cars and high-rise apartments and busybodies working hard and lowlifes not working at all. I stand ten-feet tall looming over the madness that only a place as wonderfully twisted as the big city can hold in its sadistic grasp. I frolic between towering glass buildings, skip gleefully through tunnels, past hobos, homos, junkies, and fairies, running as fast as my feet can carry through crowded roads full of yuppies with briefcases, moms pushing strollers that hold young children, as college boys and girls gather around, passing notes and chatter with one another, laughing their vivacious laughs and posing in their seductive stances, blaring horns cutting through the illuminated passageways, ecstatic traffic jams, bitter old men, crazy old women, loony and talking to imaginary friends, panhandling for their keep.... So glad to be in Boston again.

I'm home....

Appreciate everyone.

Help anyone.

Forgive someone.

Forget no one.

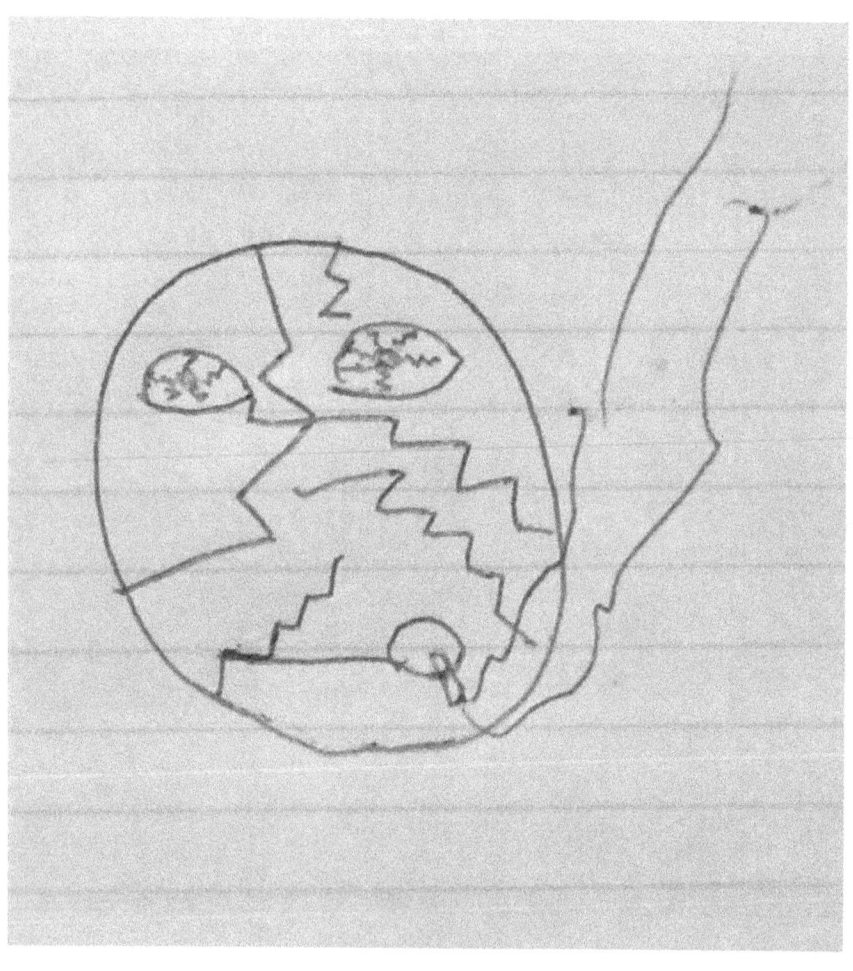

whoever said life is short is a liar

life is long ⟶ too long

in fact   it feels like forever

I could go to sleep forever and then I'll wake up and I'll never sleep again

In my writing group today I read one of my most disturbing nonfictional pieces, called "Self-Destruct," which I had found recently in my Facebook notes, and which I remember writing within days after the fact (although, now that I think about it, even though I had announced it as my most disturbing nonfictional piece, there is one, maybe two, that are a little more twisted and screwed up than that).

In said piece I mention my desire to kill said love of my life, and in my writing group one woman piped up saying, "You wouldn't actually kill her, would you? That's just strictly fantasy and speculation, correct?" I said rather curtly, "No no no, it's just fantasy and speculation, you are right." but then added: "But I have thought about killing her, this is true."
You see, love is a very powerful yet rather painful device, and although amid a love-filled affair one is showered with delight, romantic bliss, catastrophic euphoria, and the like, love can cause a torrential suffering that tears them up inside it's a terrible thing, so deeply traumatizing, and sometimes the only way out is homicide, remove your lover from the picture and you'll be all right again.

Right?

"Why not just break up with your lover, then?" she queried.

I would if I could . . . if it was really that easy—just sever your connection with the BEAST. But sometimes feelings sprout out of nothing; where there was once none, you're suddenly tethered to this man or woman and you never wanna let go and every sensation is suddenly joyful and terribly laced with sin and it feels like a shot of morphine to your heart while simultaneously being kicked in the nuts again and again and again.

That's just the nature of the beast>>>>

Everyone is crazy, everything is hazy, my lifestyle is fading away, and I feel like I'm flying. The choices I've made, and the choices I'll make, leave me feeling alone and out of place. So when all is said and done, when your life is lived and forgotten, just keep this one thing in mind: we're all living a lie, and we're all born to die. Just another condemned prisoner walking the line....

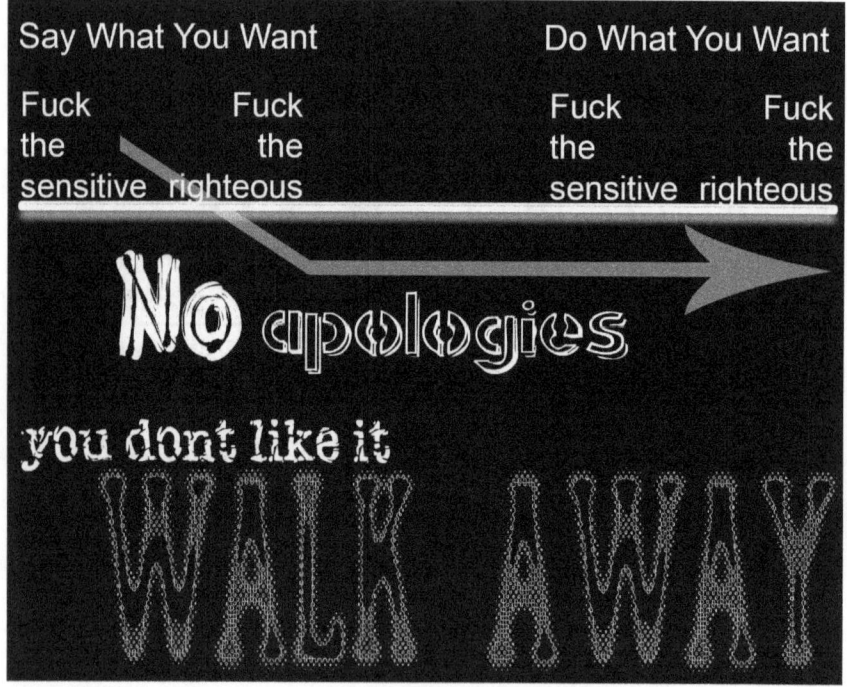

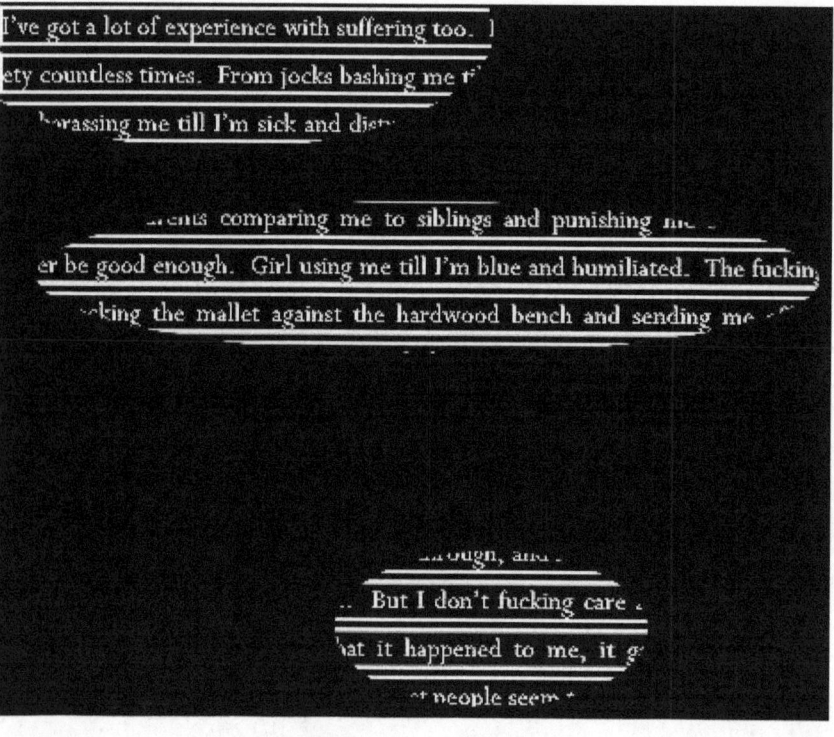

My Luck
not yours, MINE

you are NOT the luckiest guy in the world

i am

don't forget that

i'm kidding of course

you're way more luckier than i am

by a long-shot

or could it be that we're equally as lucky

do you know who isn't lucky

he and she and everyone who isn't me

and everyone who isn't you
   of course

PUNKS KILL DRUG STAR

Obituaries

"Hey, Obstacle! Go fuck yourself!"

"Why do you say that?" it says. "I'm only trying to help."

"The fuck you are. You stand in my way and try to tear me down, and you call that helping?"

"But, Jeremy Void, I love you. I only want what's best."

I smirk. "What's best, you say. What's best?? You wanna know what's best?" Pause. "Well I'll tell you what's best!" Waving my index finger around like a sword. "What's best is for you to go away—tear someone else down, why don't you! See how they like it."

My obstacle approaches. Gets in my face. Tears descending its sharp, bony cheeks.

"Go away!" I say, thrusting my index finger straight out in front of me.

I'm not gonna blindly submit to anyone, male or female. I realized earlier today that that fact gets in the way of my being in a relationship. I force people to own their own shit, and doing so forces people to own their own shit, and the only shit most people do in fact own is their denial of their own shit, and even that they deny; and I refuse to blindly submit...

Point & Click

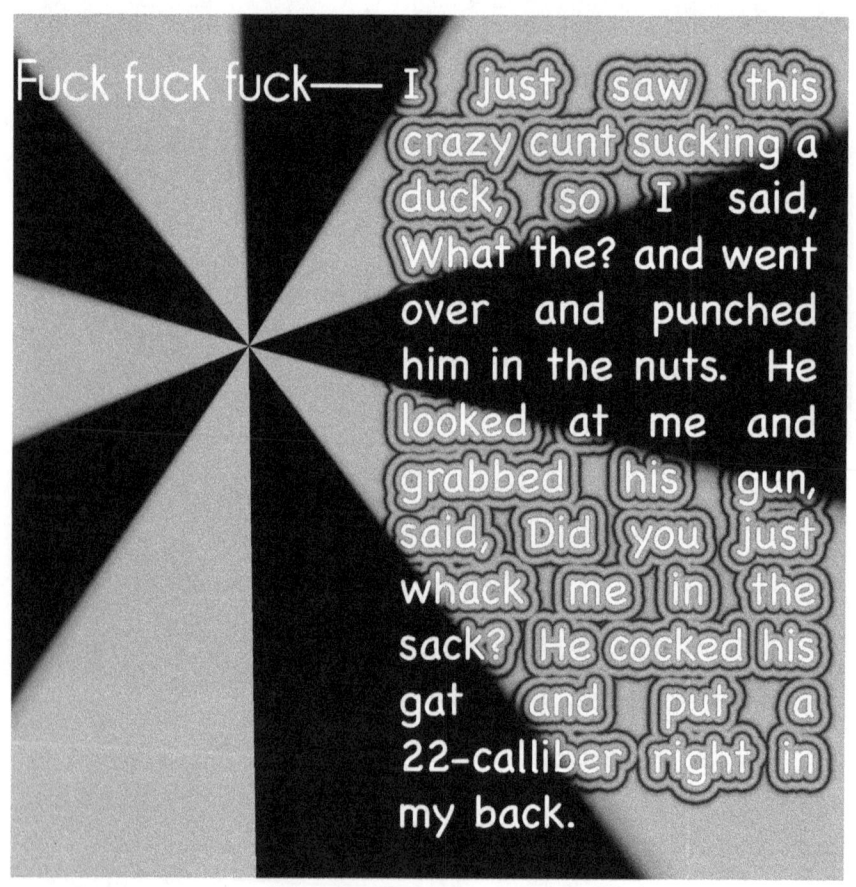

Fuck fuck fuck— I just saw this crazy cunt sucking a duck, so I said, What the? and went over and punched him in the nuts. He looked at me and grabbed his gun, said, Did you just whack me in the sack? He cocked his gat and put a 22-calliber right in my back.

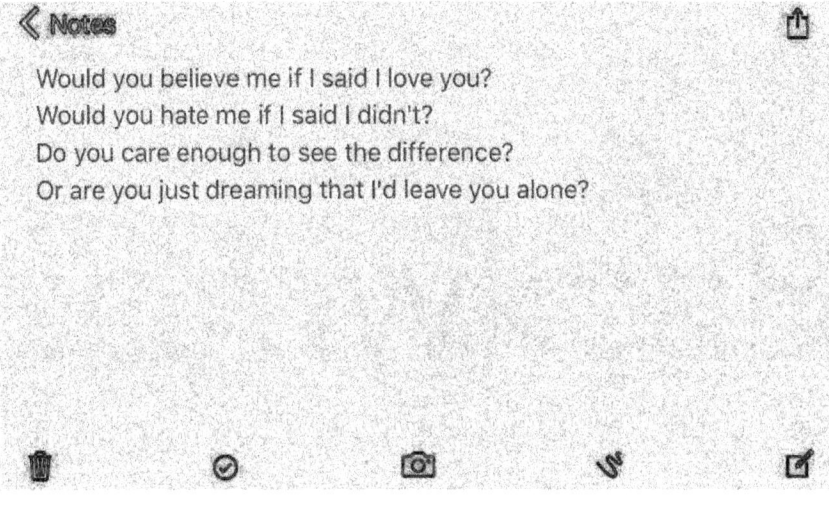

ASS Backwards

> LIVE AND LET LIVE AS LONG AS THEY LIVE IN SYNC WITH HOW YOU LIVE, is too many words. Keep it simple. LIVE AND LET LIVE is enough for me.

Jeremy Void
August 3, 2010 at 11:20pm

fuck everyone

Yes, my art has been very angry as of lately—on the darker side, even for me. Yes, it might be disturbing and even a bit creepy. But you know what, at least I'm feeling something. At least I'm making something. At least—at least—at least I'm doing something real with my life other than just pushing buttons on my phone and wasting time with a boring divergent such as this—this—THIS fucking thing, a window into "life," what life, who's life? OUR LIFE! WHAT individuality?

Who am I?
What am I?
Do I really haveta be someone??
Do I really haveta be something??

    Cuz all I really wanna be is me!

Nerds are obsessed with video games.
Jocks are obsessed with athletic fame.
Nerds do good in all their classes.
Jocks wear spandex and slap each other on the asses.

Who's the fag?
Who's the fag now?

So what if they wear glasses, you shower together.
That makes them a fag and you so much better?
You're a self-hating queer,
in denial and fear.

Who's the fag?
Who's the fag now?

Nihilism

Those nihilists that stick needles in their arms, loaded guns in their mouths, have not yet accepted the nothingness, for acceptance of the nothingness should be a liberating experience. When one finally realizes that nothing matters in the end, and the only thing relative is life and death—we are born and then we die, good fucking bye—one should not feel a fatalistic longing for life, a desire for something more; when one truly accepts that there is nothing, relieved from attachments, one should feel revived from the dead, transcending into a better world, total liberation.

For those nihilists that stick needles in their arms are rejecting the nothingness.

Death of an Artist

Oh boredom
holiest of things
I become one with
the virtue of sadness
the vice that is
a lavender painting
I paint with feces
I spit blood at the fishes
& dive into deep space
as a retro, thrummed bass
clicks like a sonic boom
it sounds like an explosion
of dust billowing up
& it's gone
& I feel pretty dumb
when a fat man plucks the magical plumb
from the tree of infinite wisdom
I feel like
I'm flying

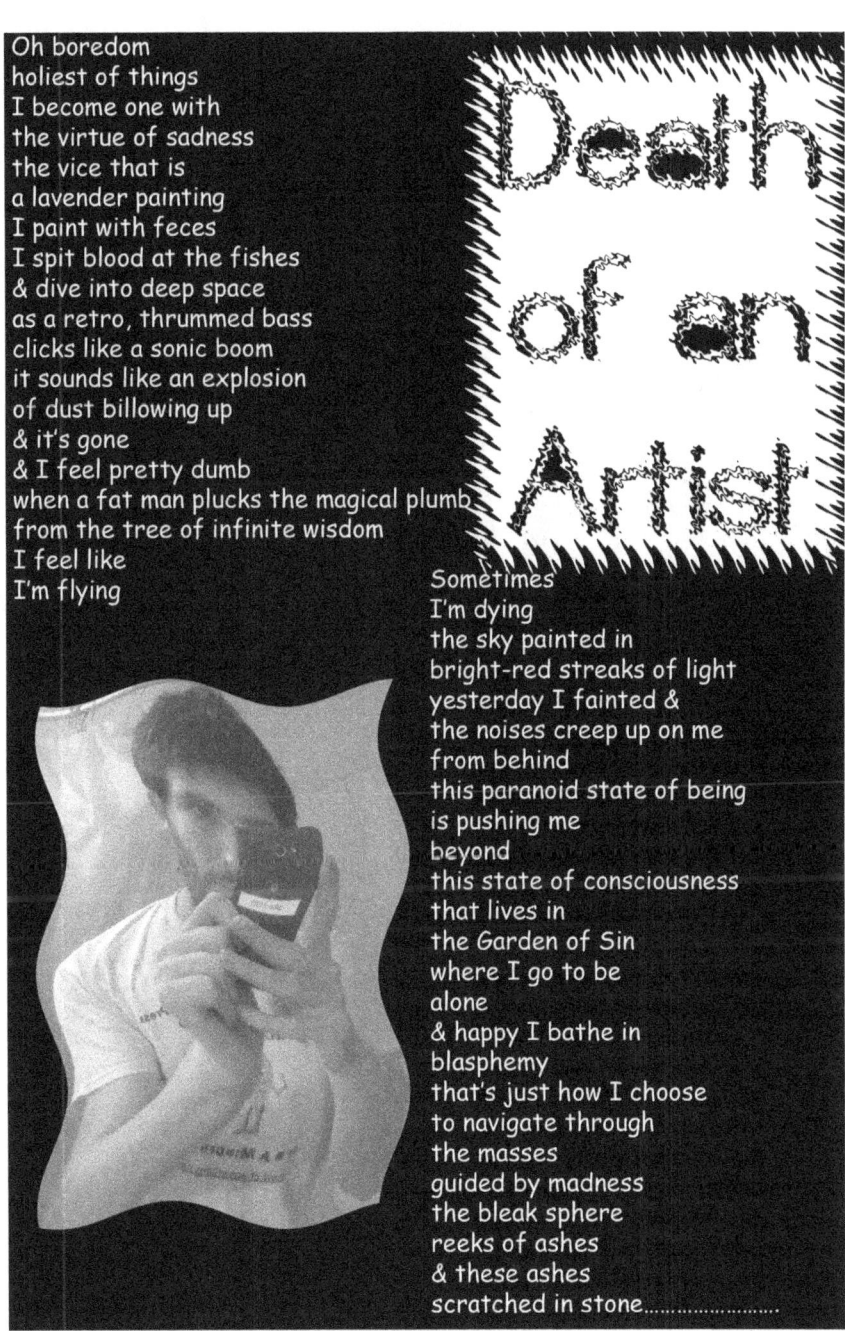

Sometimes
I'm dying
the sky painted in
bright-red streaks of light
yesterday I fainted &
the noises creep up on me
from behind
this paranoid state of being
is pushing me
beyond
this state of consciousness
that lives in
the Garden of Sin
where I go to be
alone
& happy I bathe in
blasphemy
that's just how I choose
to navigate through
the masses
guided by madness
the bleak sphere
reeks of ashes
& these ashes
scratched in stone...................

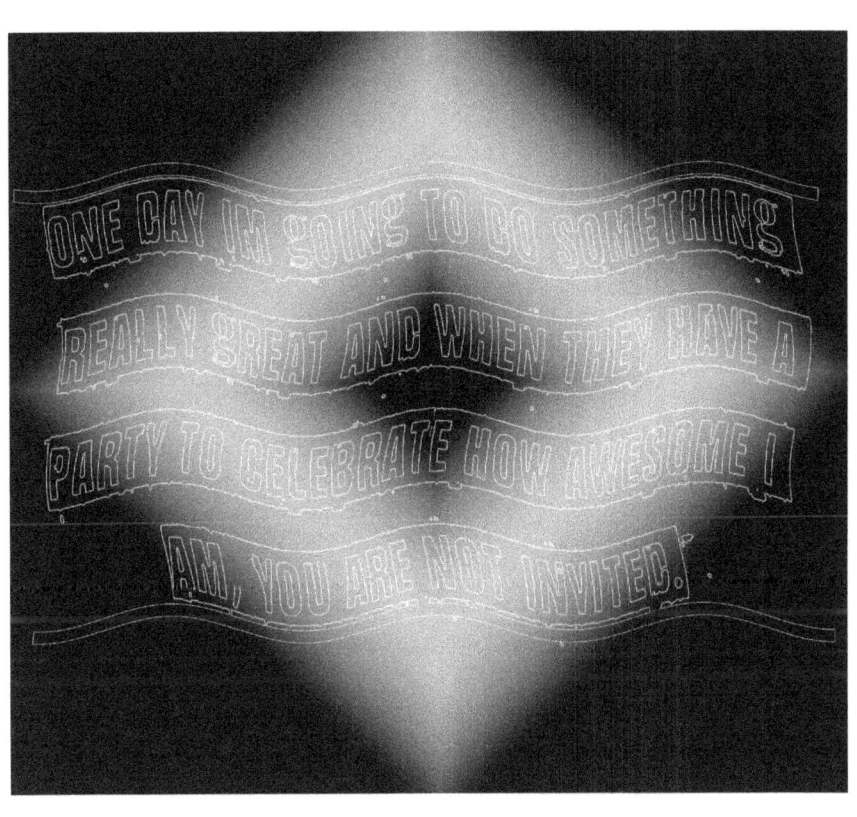

Things fall apart. Things get rebuilt. Things fall apart. Things get rebuilt. Things fall apart. Things get left abandoned. Things rot and grow mold. Things stay abandoned. Things become infested with maggots. Things stay abandoned. Things get found by mischievous teenagers. Things get covered in spray-paint. Things stay abandoned.

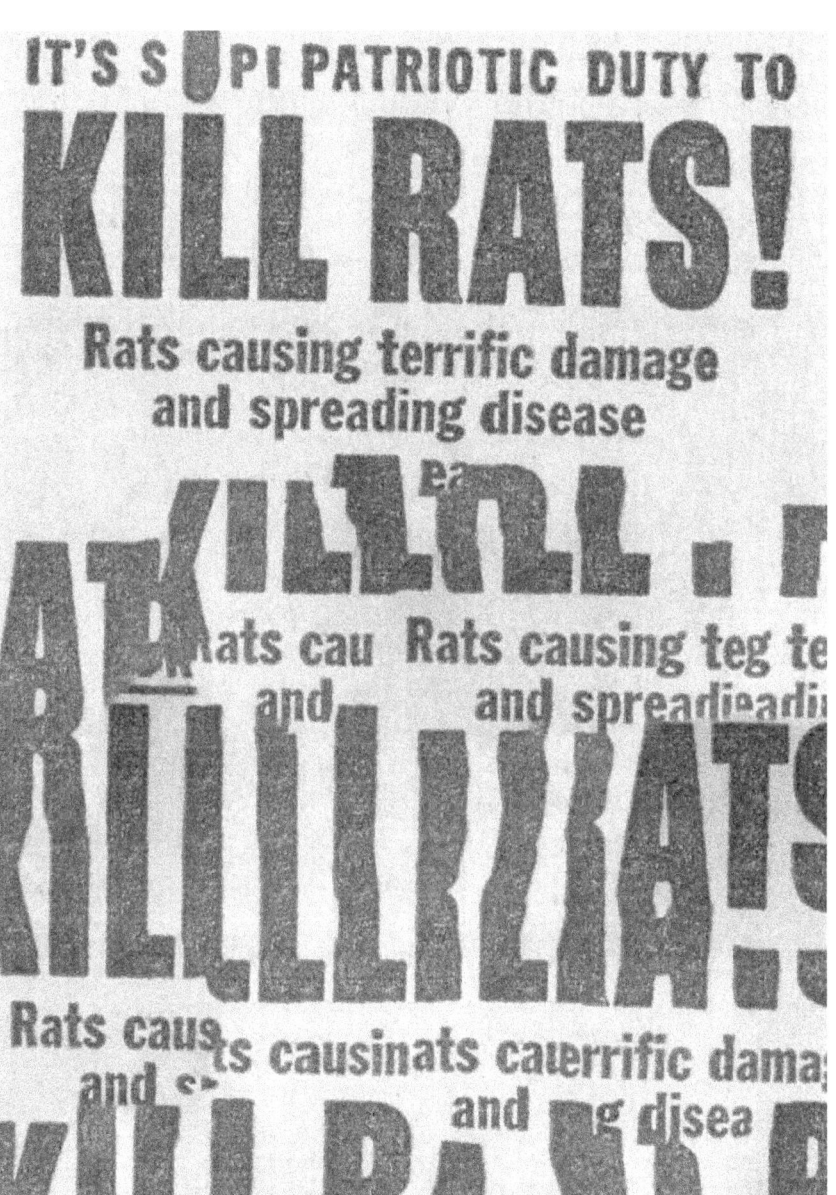

The world was black; my memories of the past seem almost surreal, like looking at a mirror with inverted color schemes and the man staring back at me, with spikey, jet-black hair and a grin of the morally defective—my arch nemesis was he. A photograph captures one's soul, but I had no soul to be captured, leaving me a hollow vessel of a man, unrecognizable and stark—a time warp into another man's life, through another man's eyes. These are my memories, but I remember them transpire in third-person through the scope of a sniper rifle.

This Is Punk Rock

Do you know why it bothers me when someone who knows nothing about Punk rock dresses Punk: it kills the camaraderie that true Punk is all about. There was a day when Punks would hold their hands out to the fallen ones. Sure, they'd ridicule you but it'd be all in fun. It's kind of ironic, but most outsiders would call Punks mean & rotten kids with no respect for anyone because we seem aggro to them with our chains & spikes & studs. But I'll tell you this: at a time when I needed a friend the most, who was it that stuck their hands out & helped me to my feet? It wasn't your own kids who look so neat in their Polo shirts & nicely ironed pleated pants. Your kids shunned me, you see, whereas Punks opened their arms wide & said, "Hey you! Kid! Fuck those little pricks! They ain't your friends! They treat you like shit! Come with us & we'll show you what friendship means; & what it means to be Punk, too. We're gonna have loads of fun, kid. Just you wait & see! Let's get outta here." So I went & I learned all about what camaraderie means, but I'll tell you, talking to these trendy kids today who look down on me through their snotty little noses, it really makes it hard to know who I can identify with & who I can't, cuz some kids just wanna look cool & feel even cooler in their black studded leather & dyed hair. You see, there is a reason for the uniform; it's so we can separate the wolves from the sheep, but today the sheep are dressed in wolves' clothing & it makes me sick, you know.

Eat the rich

obey

Kneel for the poor

It's funny how we automatically assume that those who agree with us are smart. Or at least I do. Like having the same opinion as me is a sign of intelligence.

↓ ↓ ↓ ↓ ↓

Really, having an opinion is a sign of stupidity, anyway.

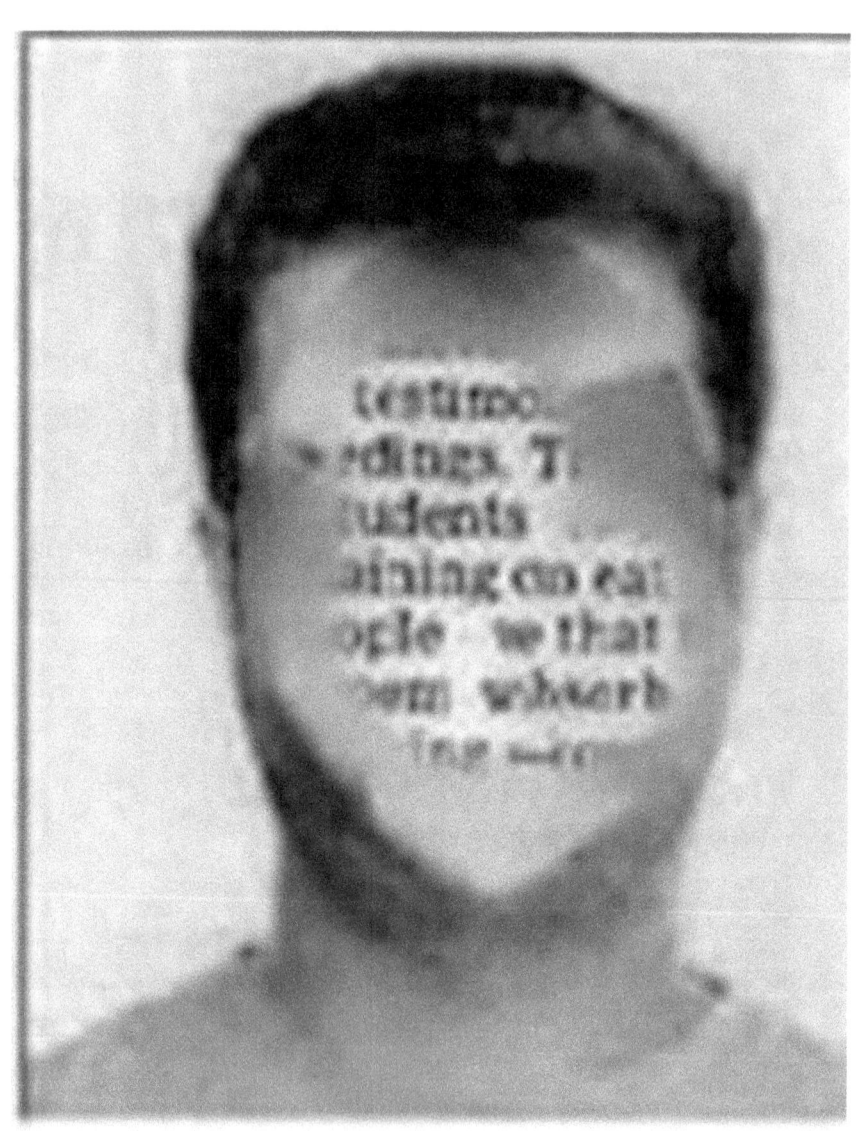

Last night I met a guy named Scott. He said he used to work at Panera Bread with me. He knew my name already, he didn't have to ask. I knew his face, but I had to ask for his name.

My past is like a puzzle with all its pieces missing, and one by one the pieces are turning up so I can finally patch it all together, although I know it will never be over, not ever....

... to be continued....

My guide says:

"You're wrong."

I say shut your pie-hole.

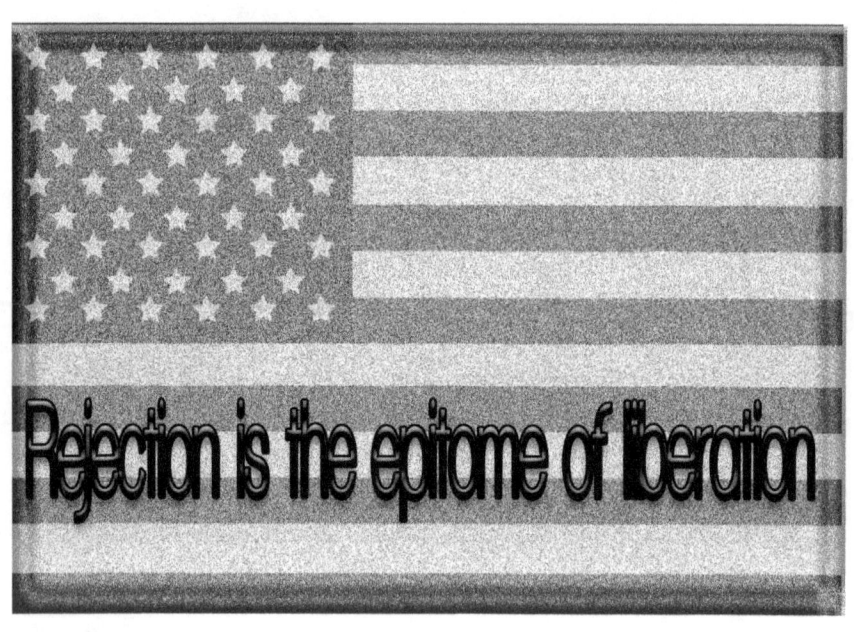

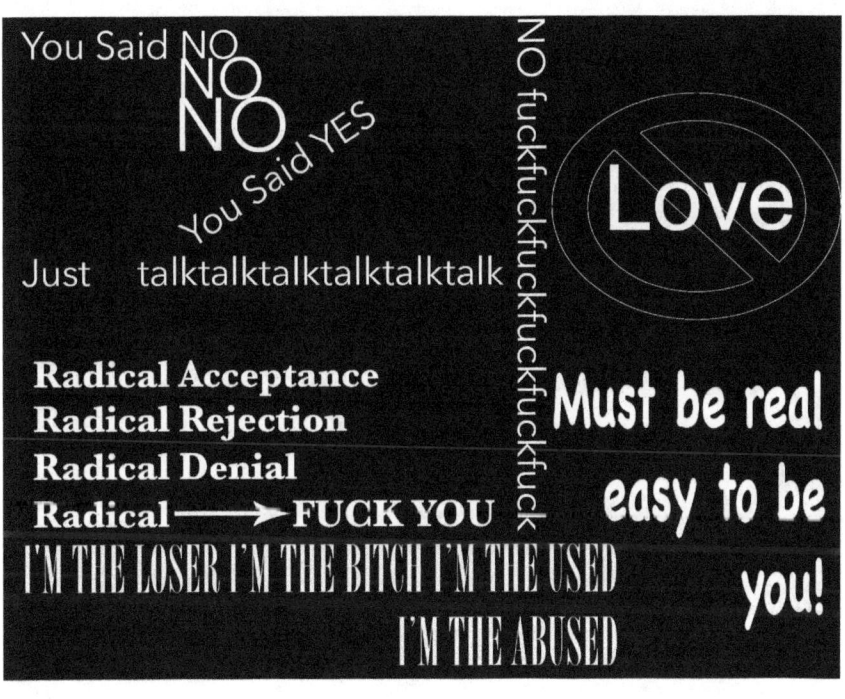

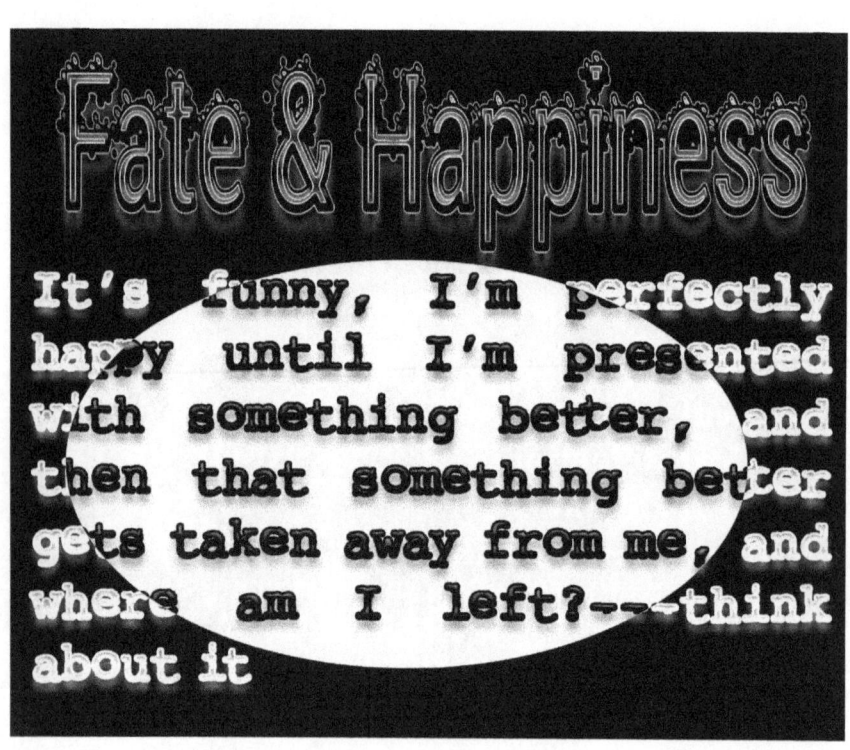

Fate & Happiness

It's funny, I'm perfectly happy until I'm presented with something better, and then that something better gets taken away from me, and where am I left?---think about it

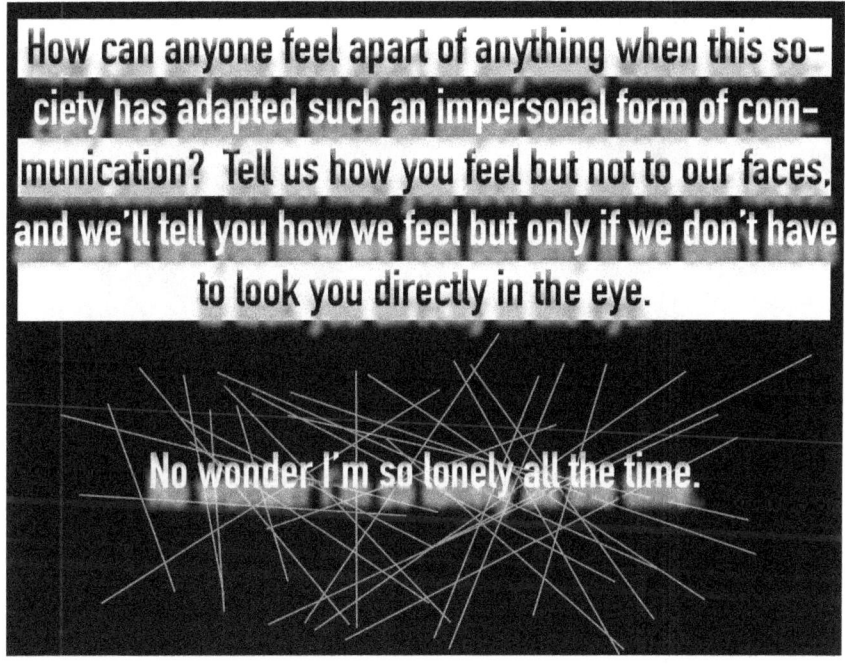

Point & Click

FROM 5 YEARS AGO:
the thought of suicide is a powerful comfort: it helps one through many a dreadful night.

I was a lot deeper back then, I think.

A philosophical pill popper I was; an esoteric drunk; a deep thinker blowing lines of speed and sticking needles in my arm. A self-destructive artist-type with an introspective bone to pick with the world. I chucked glass bottles and contemplated the meaning of breaking glass as it exploded in this universal cesspool of diarrhea that swirls in the form of ugly puss, and I wondered, I pondered, I philosophized theorized and conceptualized as the world went to hell around me and people everywhere drowned in a piss-stained, cum-tainted reality that is life---a blessed life, ain't it?

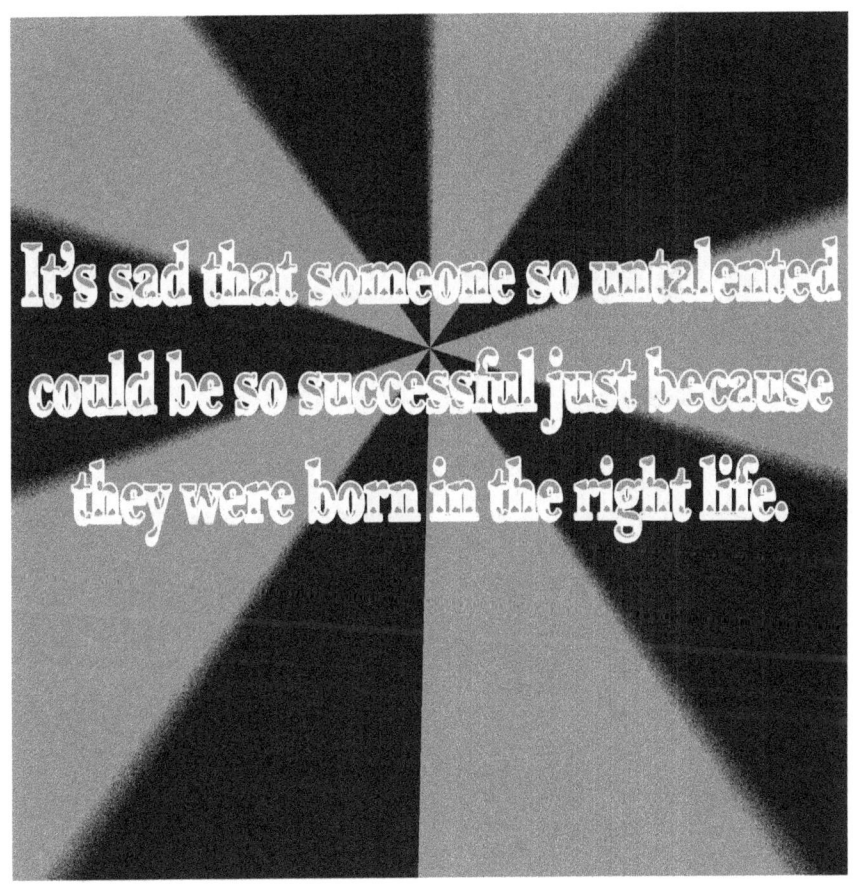

Sex Is Gay

Sex is gay.
Sex is gay.
I've just got better things to do
than go around town chasing after you.

Sex is gay.
Sex is gay.
The last place you'll find me
is in the wake of a pretty young lady.

I've lost friends.
I've lost acquaintances.
Lost so many more
to this plague of the skin.

Sex is so gay, I don't get it.

Once you come to a wall, you turn around. Driving headfirst into said wall cuz you're determined to continue going the way you wanted to go, is suicide.

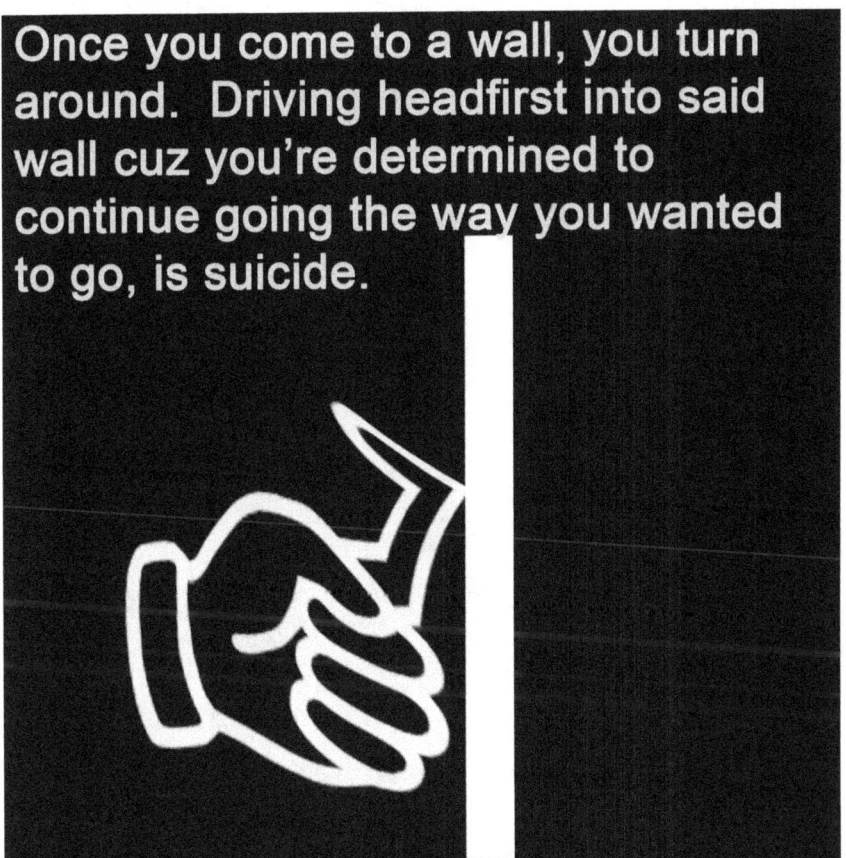

I wnta anwsers

You cant ask a liar if hes a liar, the answers you get will always come out slanted. So where does one go when they want to know the truth? not to friends & family becuz they dont wanna make you mad, not to those who hate you becuz they do wanna make you mad.

You cant trust noone becuz their opinions are always skewed by years of learned behaviors, acquired biases—— The truth is always distorted by users trying to get one over on you. The facts are always slanted by those who walk on eggshells, trying so so hard to please you. You cant trust yourself becuz your head is the number-1 offender, always spinning fabricated realities so mixed up & lost & in a world of your own.

So Where Do You Go When You Just Need to Know?

My Hell

Every girl I meet wants to fuck me, every guy I meet wants to fight me. I say things I regret but constantly tell myself I meant it. Stand strong and proud and turn the other cheek on your fellow man is my motto, and yet I'm so quick to help out the victim of persecution which I guess makes me a hypocrite, but a good hypocrite, a hypocrite who pushes negative vibes but acts nicely and kindly to everybody. I hate the nice me and wish to be the mean me but the truth of the matter is I couldn't hurt a fly, unless it bites me and then I will be the first to smash it dead. I'm a typical borderline case: I hate everybody but I'm always lonely and desperate for attention. I'm the first to tell you how much I love you, but deep down inside I hate you and want you dead, only if you died I'd miss you terribly, cuz what's the saying? Distance makes the heart grow stronger and fonder and I end up beating myself up (and off) until you're here and when I get you I toss you out the window hoping you land on your head. Ask Samantha, who I'm sure you know, all about it and she'll tell you she's been the victim of my insanity time and time again, but she loves me anyway and keeps coming back and I keep pulling her my way—except for one time, when she did the pulling for a change—and since she's so quick to forgive me all the time I feel as if she's my perfect girlfriend and I wanna marry her, unless I kill her first in which case I will cry, and cry until I meet somebody else and then I forget all about her. A week passes and everybody's gone and I'm alone and beating myself black and blue at how stupid I was for destroying such a good thing. But soon after, I find something else I can stick my dick into, stir it around like it's a pot of stew, pull out, and shoot. That's my life. Welcome to Hell!

A Bad Case of the Fuckits!

fuck the rules
fuck the law
fuck the system & everyone
who wants to bring you down
fuck it all
& tear it up
i'm bored & i'm lying
i'm living just to die
what's the point
cuz they'll all just hate you tomorrow
i ain't sold on ideas
ain't a conformist drone
ain't a machine the system's tool, a pet
just wanna be me
so fuck the world
& watch it burn
this is our life, our time
let's stand together & set it
bright on fire
i'm unhappy on the fence
i need something more than
what i'm getting
it's the day of judgment

the jury are dead
the judge is suspended
from a cherry tree
the world is ours
so let's live it up
cuz there ain't no laws
that'll catch up with us
i'm bored & i'm a victim
i'm sick of this thing called living
misery is my muse
& i hate everyone
& everything & i will see to it
that it all goes straight to hell
this country is on fire
where are the gas tanks so we can
demolish planet earth in flames
i'm bored & i'm in trouble
i think i'm seeing double
i'm sick & angry this is the day
i take a stand & say
fuck the rules
fuck the law
fuck you because
i'll do it my own way
so fuck off back to
where you belong
& leave me be
& let me have some fucking fun
before my life is done....

cuz it's all done

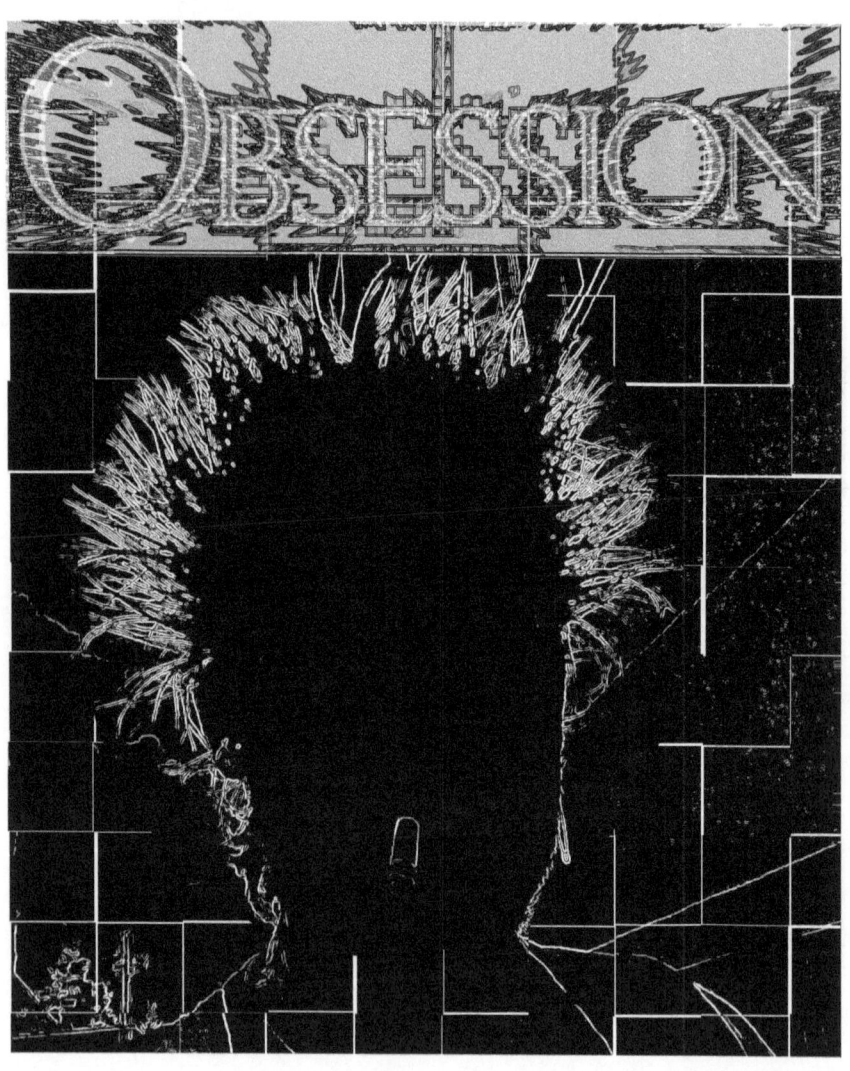

One girl said I'm not conceited enough.

Another girl said I'm too conceited.

There's just no winning when it comes to women.

Flashbacks
I read between the lies
finding myself
I'm about to take a dive.
Worrisome figures
surrounded me as I climb
the ladder into
your thighs—*forever lost in lust.*

I don't get it. All I can do is address my own side of the story and move on. I can't dwell, just assess. But I AM dwelling, but not about my side—about her side—because I don't know what that is. How will I ever know if she wants nothing to do with me? I've destroyed many relationship I've been in; I know when I'm wrong, and I'll usually fess up to it right away, just like how I had showed up at her doorstep one night to apologize for everything I had done to her. It's funny though, the more I got to know her the more I realized how completely full of shit she was. This problem has been over and done with for many months now, but still my brain comes back to this issue every now and then. I've fucked up my own share of relationships, but even after addressing my own side, all the arrows point toward one thing and one thing only >>> HER. I've fucked up plenty of relationships, but in this particular one I was not the one who turned and threw it all away. I did the right thing every step of the way. Yeah, I made a few mistakes too, I'll admit; but I fessed up to them, which she seemed to lack the ability to do. I can't blame anyone for my own actions, all I can do is learn to fix them so I don't repeat them; but still my brain, every now and then, circles back to this; and all I want to know is WHY. So that I can move on.

I'm sitting in a crowd, of a few old men, they talk but I don't hear what they say. Their minds like eyes, their eyes like spies, their voices cold as ice & sharp as a knife. I sit here in this great world & wonder things that only the drunken cloaked woman lurking in the dark & dank shadows can understand, comprehend, & she scoffs & scowls in that bleak tone that sounds like a revving motorcycle as the angry rider kicks the pedal & cranks the handles.

This is my life, coming to terms with nothing, trying to understand something, learning anything my small mind can comprehend with its midget legs & arms of a giant that reach & reach & reach but the legs are too stubby & they get stuck in cement & the arms keep reaching & reaching but my brain feels heavy & I give up & go to sleep instead.

This foreign world seems so ordinary to me, like been there done that, & yet it feels so different & I find myself on an indifferent playing field, wanting something more but something seems to bore me & I find my mind slipping as my eyes seize up & I fall asleep in the shower as the plummeting spray bounces off the edge of my skull & the tub is closing in on me fast, getting tighter, & the lights are brightening & opening holes in my head, so as to spray me with this relentless kind of knowledge that seems almost insufferable, & I pray to no one asking for relief. But then the relief comes to me unexpectedly & I look up at the clouds—the churning, shifting, & spurning webs of fluffy fog that puff out & fold over—& I marvel at the magical undulations of the spacious skies & for once this life makes a little more sense to me & that something that lurks up there comes into focus & I find satisfaction in such a bleak world & I walk away with my head upright
only to get shot down around the corner by a jagged spike of lightning that came from below & that seems to be the story of my life.

So I'm sitting in a crowd of a few old men, listening to their chatter come like waves of sonic might, & I hear their voices which sound like churning rice & I watch & observe, basking in the wisdom of a thousand years of abuse, absorbing the worldly trinkets of information that seem quite foreign but still so ordinary, & I think to myself, This is life, this is good, & for once I understand what it means to be bad & I understand the crashing collision of stumbling over a bed of rocks & stones & ruts & that precious bite as the rocks rip into your skin & for once in my horrible existence I see the glorifying truth & I'm falling & I'm wondering plummeting & crashing into stacks of romantic bliss & I'm not looking back. And I'm having a blast. And I'm running from the law with my one-eyed widowed girlfriend who holds a knife to my back. It's over I know.

It's over & my whole life has only just begun....

Gone Astray

What the fuck is going on?? Never thought I'd be on this side of things. That I'd be the one who cared. A couple hours ago I get a phone call. My friend has gone missing. It was his mom. She's a nervous wreck. Worried he might die. Who could blame her? I've even thought the same. Wanted to text him the other day to say why don't you just stick the gun in your mouth. Quit playing God. Pull the trigger, why don't you! Stop us from guessing. The anticipation of the last hit. The final spike that will end it all. STOPPIT, Goddammit!

I sit at the library. I try to read. My thoughts are firing. I'm so worried. For my friend. For his mom. Never thought I'd be on this side of things. Worried for another man's life. Turn the page. Gives Rock Bottom a new meaning, right? The AA meeting starts soon. In three minutes.

I scratch my balls. I scratch my pen across the page. Chicken-scratch—it's all the same. Ride the waves. Smooth sailing. But it isn't smooth. Not by a long-shot. Never thought I'd be here. In Rutland. In the Rutland free library. Waiting for the AA meeting to start. Stoppit, Goddammit. Stop the pain. Are you happy. Are you having fun?

Pull the trigger and see what happens. I'm not having fun. Losing control. Is he all right? Am I all right? Never thought I'd be on this side of things. Never thought I'd be... all right.

Pull the trigger and see what happens. Everything's going to be fine....

Oblivious Discontentment

I noticed something wasn't quite right. I stared out the window at the lashing flames that whipped and thrashed and devoured everything in sight. What the hell is wrong with this picture? I mused, as the window exploded and broken glass assaulted me head-on, nipping and stabbing exposed skin. I stood there and mulled over this new development, trying so hard to figure out the root of the problem.

With a cataclysmic crunch a large maple tree snapped in half leaving only a crude-looking stump in its passing, and with that my whole house shook and the lights flickered and the room went suddenly dark, the only light coming from the shuddering fire outside the broken window.

Should I call someone, maybe?

"Wendy!" I yelled.

"What?" rasped my wife from upstairs.

"Are you seeing this?"

"What?"

"Outside, honey. Are you seeing what's happening?"

"I'm sleeping. You woke me up."

"Sorry, honey. Go back to bed. It's not that big of a deal, anyway."

I could feel the fire singeing the hair on my head; I rubbed my chin. *Hmm.*

Something didn't feel quite right, was all I knew.

Is anybody listening to me? Can anybody relate with me? Can you identify, put yourself in the picture, or am I so strange and my ideas so foreign that I come across as unreal, sad, pathetic, crazy. Lost. YOU'RE RIGHT I AM FUCKING LOST. Lost sick & fed up. The rage is roiling. My thoughts are boiling. The stew is overflowing. And I'm coming after you. Guns blazing.

Haha——it's all just a dream.

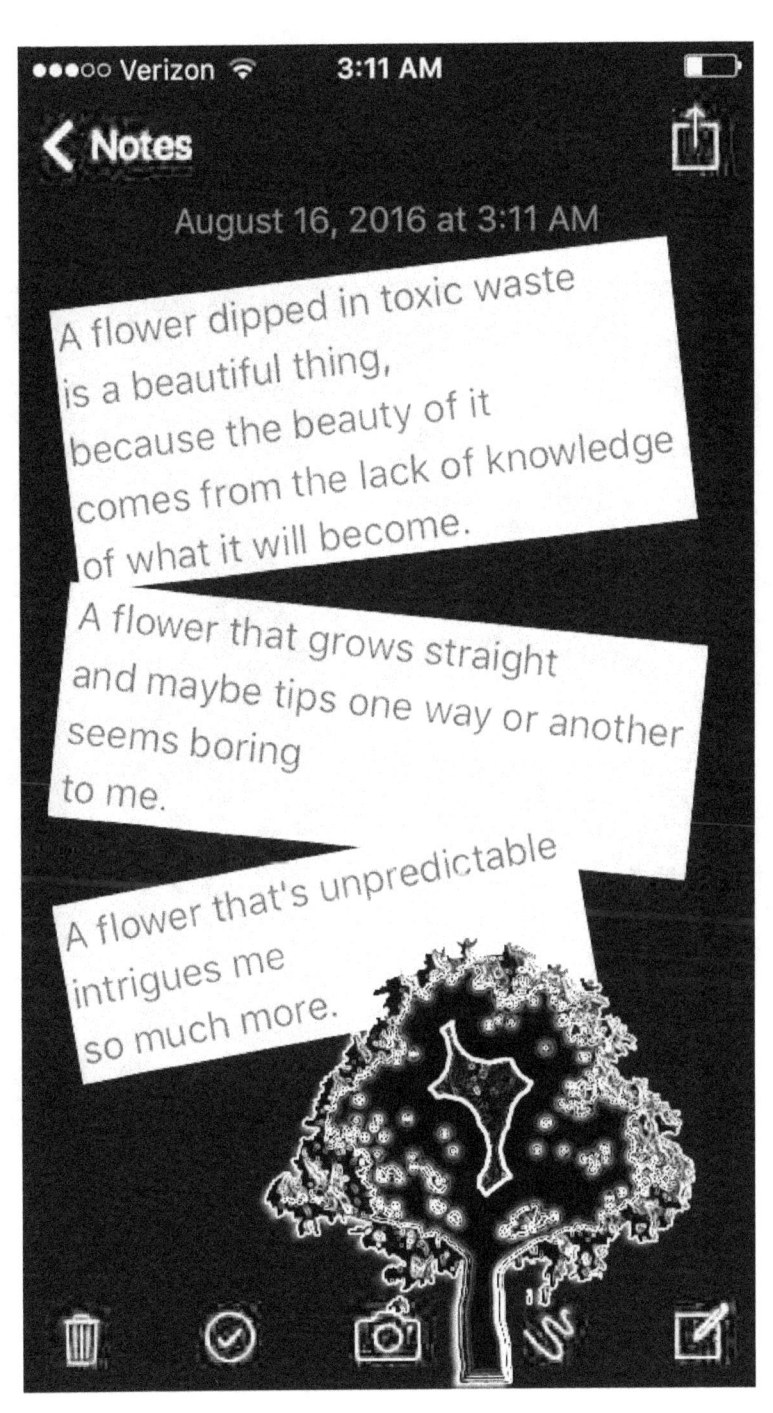

Perfection is a disease, but not in the sense that we become perfect when infected. But rather, we seek it like vampires after blood. It's a disease of the mind and body, it reaps havoc on those who do not have it. But defective is a blessing. Acceptance of your follies is the greatest gift anyone can ever get. When you look in the mirror and see a beautiful disproportionate oblong figure smiling back at you, now that's something to strive for.

I don't mean to interrupt you, but my random thoughts and memories are much more important than what you are talking about— because if you were a little more interesting of a speaker I wouldn't be thinking about other stuff in the first place.

Everyone Is a Cunt

Everyone is a cunt, with no exceptions.
I'm a cunt, you're a cunt, he's a cunt, and she's—

Wait, would that be sexist?

times are changing &
everyone & everything
is moving forward & i'm
being left behind.

things change, but i'd
imagine that i'd change
with them.

A Life-Span of Five Hundred Thousand Light Years

Blow a fuse
and see how far it'll take you.
Run backwards on ice
as the devil watches and the mold
comes back for round 2.
A Vacuum is a fantastic vacation spot
a void the size of my head
rotting out from the inside.
A Blackhole—
wash yourself with monkey blood
look through the eyes of a four-legged vampire
stick your middle finger through the hole
located at the center of the earth
and then shout as loud as you can:
THERE IS A WORLD IN WHICH I HAVE YET
TO WATCH EXPLODE IN TEARS DRIPPING FROM
THE BRIGHT RED EYES OF A NAKED WOMAN'S LUSTFUL
WAYS!!!
You know, there is a lot to do when
you're only 3-inches tall and everyone is a giant.
And the world is your apple orchard
and you run amok through a world divided
by virtuous princesses stealing crowns ...
off the heads of a thousand mini mountains.

I think I'm manic right now—just a bit.

Who wants to see my nipples?

Found my old iPhone last night, and in doing so I got to read some of the texts I had sent the day I had lost it. Basically I was really, REALLY manic at the time—and I'm thinking now that I had hid the phone on myself just so that I would stop sending these stupid texts to certain people, but then I completely forgot about that seconds later when I had the impulse to send another stupid text, because that's the only explanation I can think of of how my phone ended up in the place that it had ended up in. But, anyway, I read some of the texts last night, and boy was I crazy that day; some of them didn't even make any sense, they were complete fucking gibberish—haha, WTF!

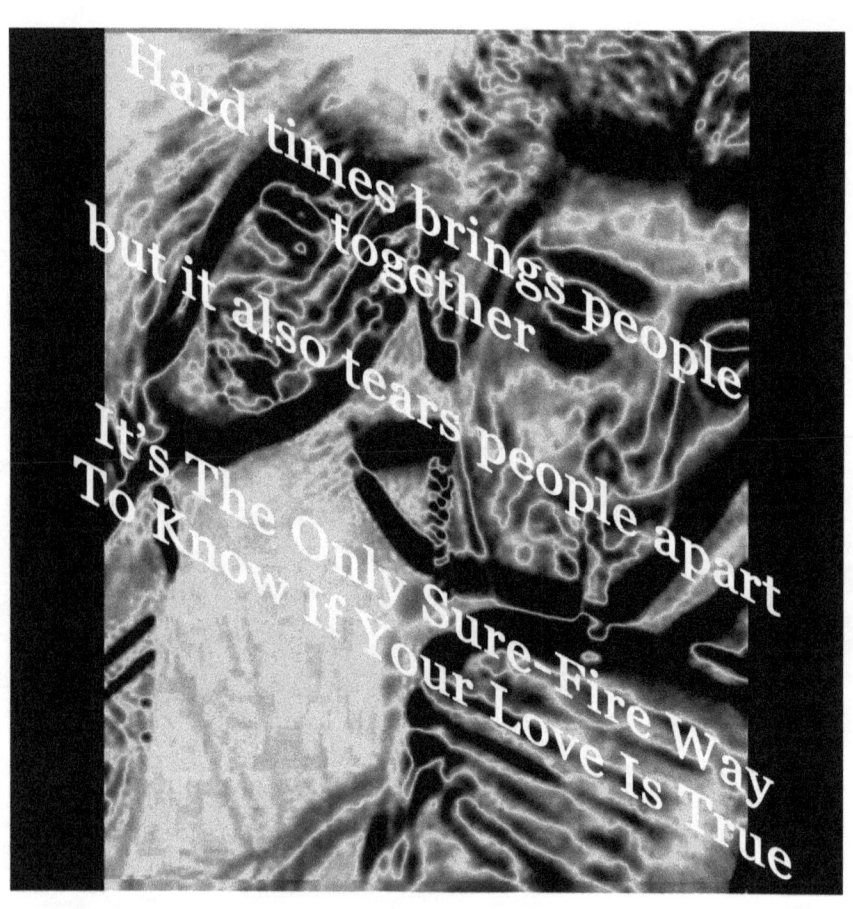

Life was fast and I spent some time behind bars. I remember back when running from the police was an afterschool hobby. Hopping fences and darting through backyards, with red and blue lights burning holes in the night and sirens wailing as my feet slapped in puddles, as I cut through one alley after another.

I was a scumbag. I was a lowlife. I lived with one goal in mind, to die young and leave an ugly corpse. I wanted people to spit on my decrepit body. I wanted to be seen as a hero to a small few and a villain to the rest, but simply put I was an anti-hero. I stole from the rich and kept for me and my friends.

The stereo would blaze our nightly terroristic haze. Running from the law while good old-fashion Punk rock played loud and fast as the nightly theme. Maybe the "Anti-Nowhere League" with "Let's Break the Law" or Blood for Blood's "Chaos."

Windows shattered, tires spewed air as I retracted the blade and we were off running again.

Chucking pumpkins through windows on Halloween, fighting the bad fight with good old whiskey on our sides.

Knives and chains tangled by our sides as we trekked through the city…. on a seek and destroy mission, carving our marks like battery acid on everything in our paths….

I guess I had fun…. to say the least.

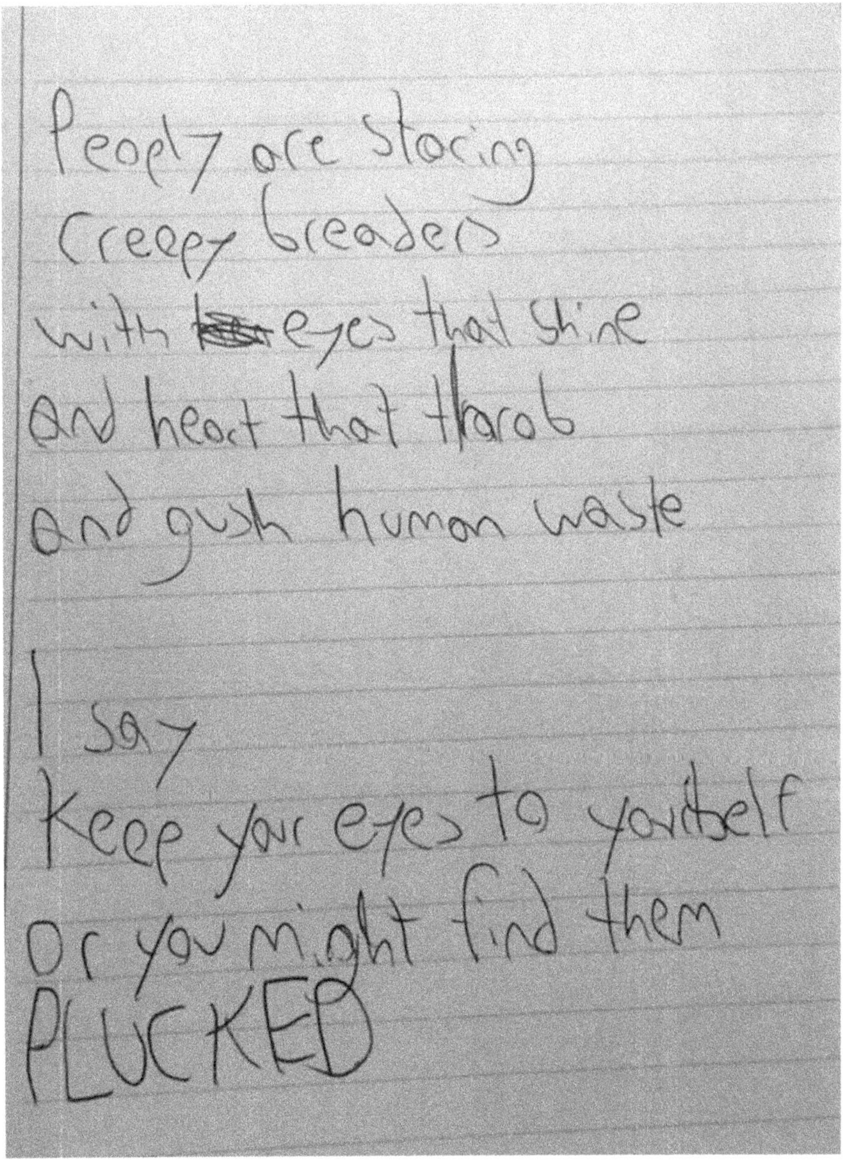

People are staring
creepy breaders
with ~~be~~ eyes that shine
and heart that throb
and gush human waste

I say
Keep your eyes to yourself
or you might find them
PLUCKED

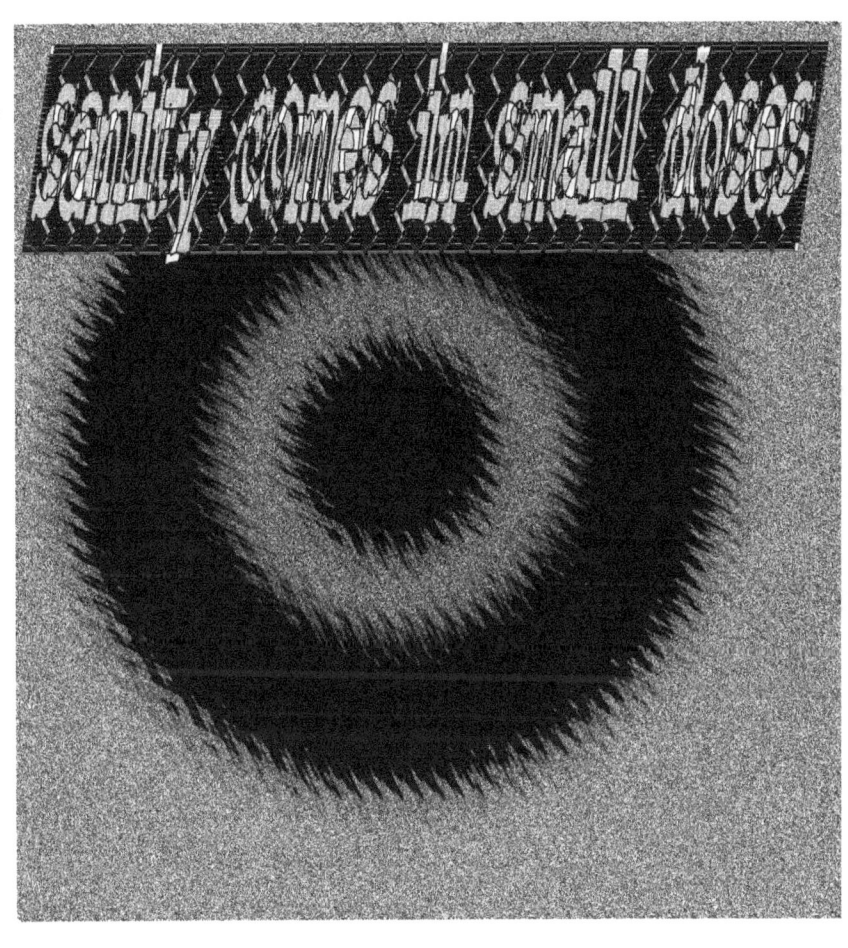

My heart is like dynamite

when it gets too hot, it EXPLODES

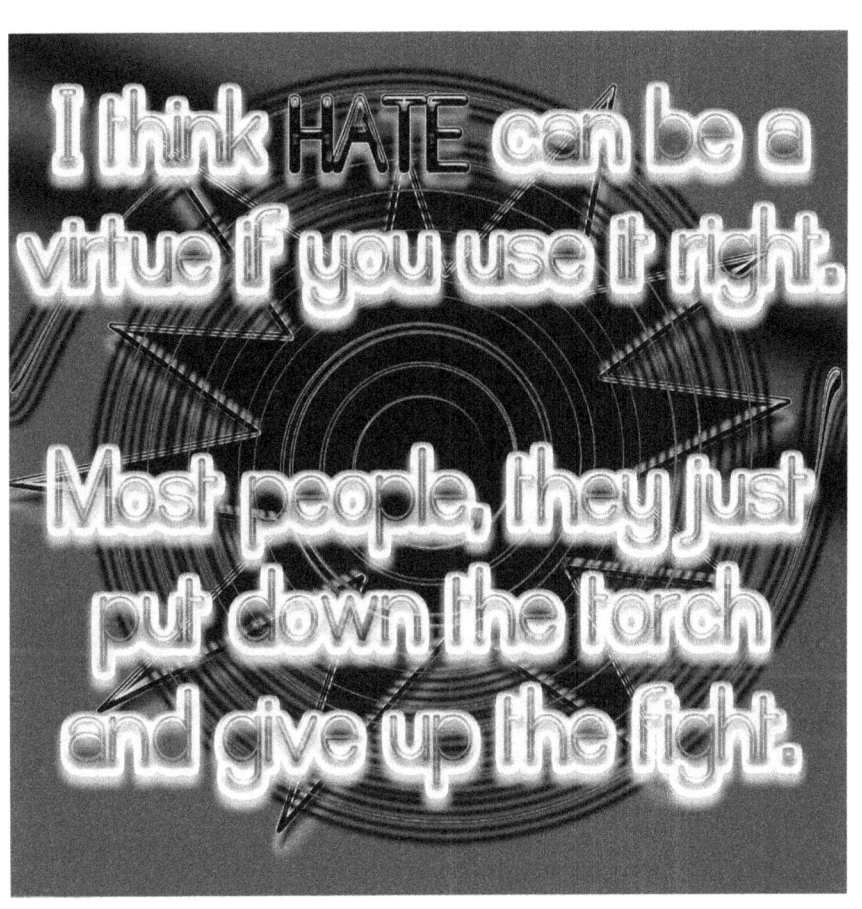

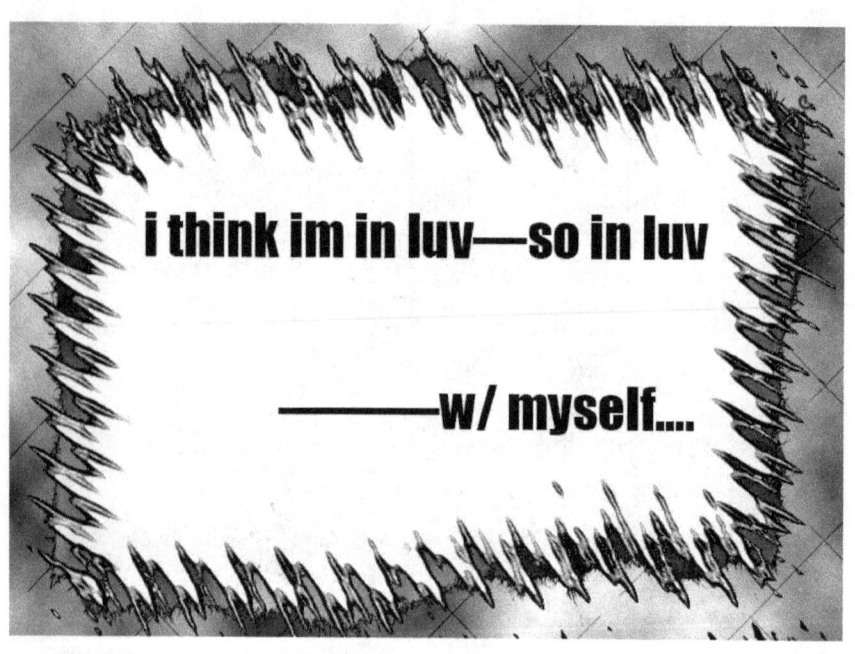

Fuck the Chaffee

we're Guerrillas

Pdionara

LIVE Like There's No Tomorrow

I was just thinking of the concept "Don't do anything you'll regret," because I saw that someone had said it in regards to a painting with suicidal ideations. (I know the guy who painted it and he's not suicidal in the least, just playing around with ideas, is all.) Once you die, you die; it's over. No regrets, no remorse, no nothing; just blackness. Sure, there might be heaven and hell, but in this story there isn't—there's nothing. So, how one would regret suicide is beyond me. I hope everybody IS doing stuff they regret, because at least they're alive to regret it.

I'm a Poser—so what?

It's like, everybody's a hypocrite, right? In which case I'd much rather own my own hypocrisy than go around believing the lie that I'm better than that. So last night when the girl said she wasn't a poser, I couldn't help but laugh. You see, we're all posers, squandering this universe in search of ourselves, lost and troubled—nobody knows who they are in the end, we're all sick and crazy and so utterly LOST, and nobody is better than this - - than that——nobody is immune to the human disease.... It's called living in a commercialized existence, a world run by corporate giants and these bullshit advertisements on the TV, on the INTERNET, looming over the highway—everywhere you go, there's an ad trying to sell you IPods, McDonald's, a brand-new television set so that you won't miss all the latest advertisements as the corporations beam them into your skull through Blue Tooth technology. It's impossible to not be lost, it's why I avoid TV, I don't watch movies, and I don't follow the news - - - - but still, they're trying to sell you cereal that gives you aids with each mouthful. I'm lost, I'm a poser, I'm hopelessly devoted to destroying myself.... So fuckin what????

What the hell have you done??

Point & Click

Victoria was a queen who created a social order as a way to dominate Great Britain. Instead of enforcing a proper etiquette, she had the people stand up and do it for her.

Sound familiar?

Don't ask me

I'm no writer

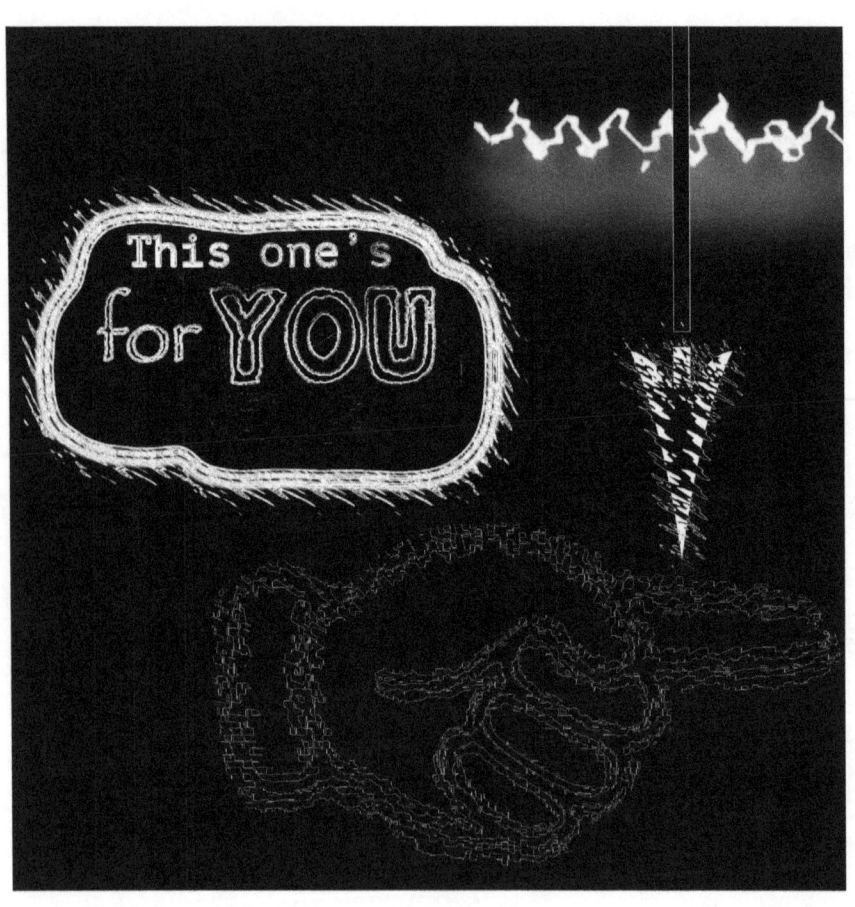

CONVERSATION
I wanna talk to you until your head explodes

, humdrum boring people transforming themselves into pseudo-elves, and will stay that way mingrm mingrmir
nse , thems selves ito
Dorin ill staemselves into th um
emsel that
nse es ins int into into into
D
umdrum
g theole

A Free-Write///

It's a free-write in my Thursday writing group. It's only me & Ted here, Barry didn't show; he's up on the hill, said Dick Thompson. So we're here writing. I read Ted a few pieces from *Smash a Lightbulb: Poetry for Lowlifes* with the hope to pull some topics of discussion out of his twisted mind. First I thought pleasure—pleasure drives me insane ("This orgasm is too much to take at this present moment," was the prompt I came up with))). Second I thought obsession (I'm obsessed with pleasure / obsession is pleasurable— —it climbs into my brain and fucks me senseless from the outside-in—the inside-out—upside-down and all around me a static pressure surges lifting me straight up into outer space))). *C'mon Ted, think of a topic,* I pressed. *Anything, Ted. You're good at that.* Me, my topics are always dirty—crude, rude, & lewd—but not today: he has nothing, no idea no concept no head on his shoulders which produces thought-provoking (or thought-REvoking, depending on which way you look at it), evocative concepts that rattle my chain,,, whip me till I'm blue and confused,,, hold me down and hock loogies in my face. (The other day in Boston I was at my friend Gary's place and I told him and Bell the story of when the kid had told me not to spit on him; comes up to me rather rudely and says, "I hear you've got a reputation for spitting on people while your band plays" [I was the singer], and adds: "Don't spit on me!" So during our set I called him up to me and hocked a loogy in his face. When I told this to Gary and Bell they both said he was asking for it. When I told this same story to a crowd of four or five at the show in Providence, RI, a few days later, one guy said he would have socked me in the face; another guy concurred; at the table a guy and a girl laughed as these two big guys joked about how if someone had hawked a loogy in one of their faces, unless accidentally discharged while coughing, they'd both deck him, right off the bat, no questions asked. I chimed in: "I'd hump his leg<<<")

So it's a free-write, Ted had declared.

For a long time I did everything for myself, and at the time I was very confident and I knew what I wanted and what I believed in. Today it seems I do EVERYTHING for everyone else, and I don't know, I seem to be lost, unsure, broken, and hurt.... I don't know what I want and I don't know how to get it. Just give give give and I'm sick of giving. I wanna be me, but I forgot what that means. I wanna live free, but you know, I don't see that happening any time soon. I'm in a box, and I can't get out. PEOPLE are stuffing me in boxes with their boring assessments of me and it's no use trying to prove them wrong because every attempt at that will only be interpreted as something I never meant. I'm claustraphobic and this figurative box is closing in and getting tighter around me. STOP FUCKING JUDGING ME, STOP ASSESSING ME, STOP THINKING ABOUT ME, I don't need anymore tension to hold me in place. I've got enough tension of my own keeping me locked inside this fate. I WANNA ESCAPE, I WANNA ESCAPE, I wanna fucking escape. You're all killing me in the dark. It's useless, anyway.

I wave to just about everyone I see while walking down the street.

I remember once——and I only remember this because I wrote about it in my very first journal about four years ago——two girls were walking by me and they waved. WAVED. Two preppy girls who didn't look like the type that would wave to me. They waved, and I thought it so weird.

This big-shot NYC editor gave a lecture about how you shouldn't combine action and depth (which is what makes up the classics of literature, she said). The best kinds of stories, according to her, have both those ingredients, but it's nearly impossible to pull it off. Hmm, I thought. So I asked her if she would like to read one of my stories, and she ran away from me. She ran away, I found out later, because I would have had to pay seventy dollars to speak to her one on one. I only wanted her to read "The Haunted Bathroom," is all.

Lack of bodies doesn't prove there's no serial killer: Expert

Chances are I'll be up all night editing and doing other random tasks that involve wasting time and procrastinating and waiting for the world to end, etcetera etcetera, and if you're looking for me, look in the mirror, you might find me there. Just say Jeremy Void three times backwards, or forward, I don't think it matters....

An Ideal

I know who I am, but if I told you, you'd think I'd be lying.
Some people think I'm hard.
I know who I am, but if I told you, you'd think I'd be lying.
Some people think I'm soft.
I know who I am, but if I told you, you'd think I'd be lying.
Some people think I'm cold.
I know who I am, but if I told you, you'd think I'd be lying.
Some people think I'm hot.
I know who I am, but if I told you, you'd think I'd be lying.

The Bleak Shopping Mall

Sitting outside the bleak shopping mall at night watching the stars twinkle in the distance as the daytime lights up the streets like wildfire & cars a riffraff of death & destruction in arms.

There was something special about the aloneness,
but now I find myself towering over townhall from a sharp, stony peak—the sunlight like gunfire, a green yard glowing, voices penetrating the nothingness that is
here
now
I'm alone
I'm dead
I'm alive
but overfed
zeroing in on the NOTHING

A bleak reality
meek existing
dripping pen ink
down the unicorn's back—
see what I mean?

The bleak shopping mall at war with the junky's sunken eyeball, the world overrun & deserted....

The bleak shopping mall stands tall above everything else, so derelict & desolate, & I sit there watching as life spreads like a virus. It spreads & devours, the sun murders the beautiful dark heavens.

If you catch me sleep-walking please lead me off a cliff!

What is wrong with me?

A really nice girl said she wanted to hang out with me sometime and in response I said something rude and uncalled for.

It's in my experience that people who claim to be smart are usually not, people who claim to be mature are usually fairly immature, people who claim to know who they are are usually the farthest away from an understanding of self. I'm not smart, I'm definitely not mature, and I definitely do not know myself like I wish to. I am an impulsive hypocrite, I talk shit and put people down, I spit, I swear, I eat with my mouth open, sometimes I'm scared of my own shadow, I'm quite the idiot at times, but there are other times, although rare, that I can be quite sincere. but in those time of me being honest and real for a change I'm honesty thinking about how to evade you for the rest of my life because you are a lazy bore and you mean nothing to me.... I'm a loser, a scoundrel, I cash checks that I surely cannot catch. I have a bone to pick with the world because the world has turned against me and the world has turned against me because I turned against it and I turned against it because I was bored of waiting for the light to turn green, see what I mean. I'm lazy and ignorant, I talk big and move slow, I run with wolves who despise me and I despise them because we're one big family of spiteful cretins looking out for numeral uno, stashing knives behind our backs as we wait for the precise moment to stab our brothers and sisters in the backs. I am not smart, I am not mature, and I, me, this man typing this rant on this filthy laptop at this very minute, am a stranger to myself..........

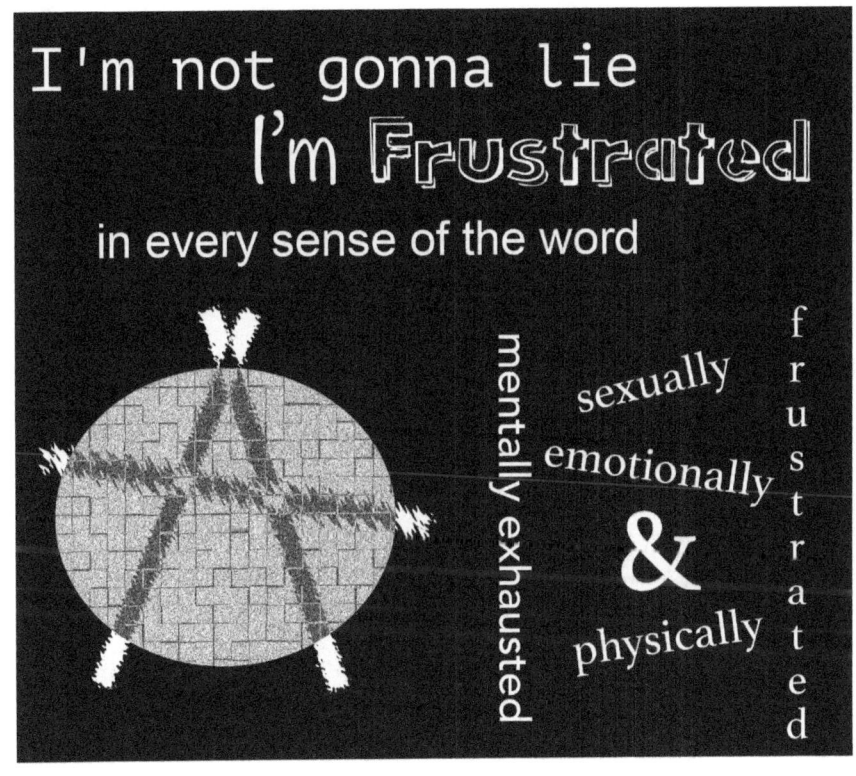

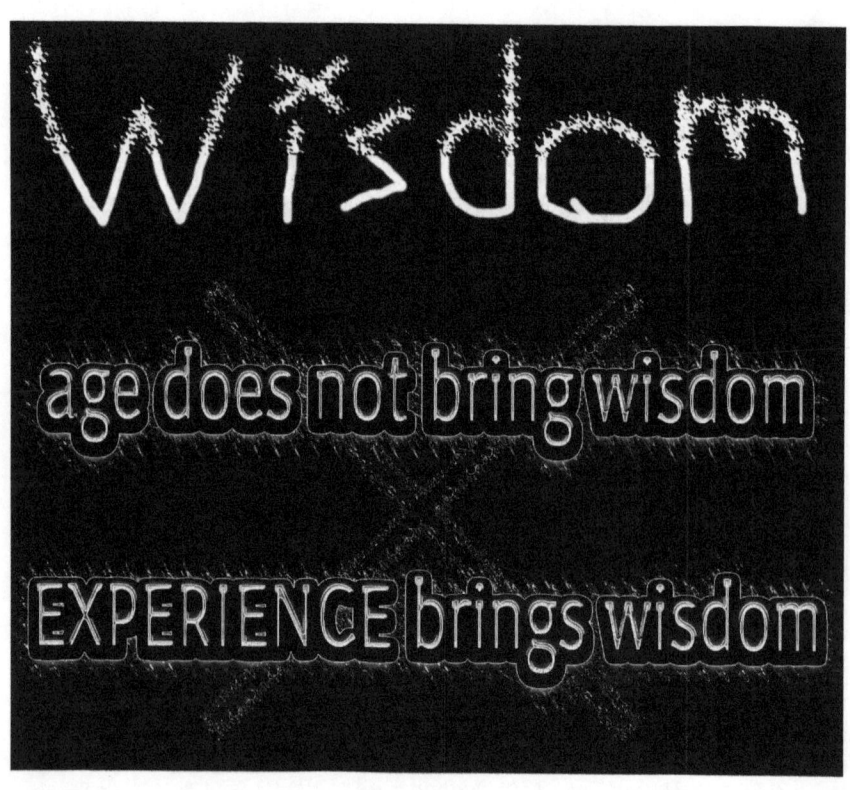

Wow, I saw that coming—
People are so predictable sometimes.

It's the morning, I've gotta slow my brain some, maybe with a stream of words as they pour from my fingertips and rack the keyboard to tap out letter after letter, and it's the morning.

It's the morning, I made it through the night, I'm alive but barely. I'm restless and I'm scattered and my brain is a mishmash of images and I'm lost in an endless torturous fucked-up chain of thought. Get me out of this cage before I take your name down with me on my plunge, grip the wall, grip the ceiling, I'm flailing and kicking and screaming, and it's the morning.

Anyway, where was I? Didn't sleep last night, filled up my mind with retarded things and now I'm here to transcribe it for you. It's the morning and I feel so useless. Anyway, where was I?

One night down, a lifetime of more to go—the morning has a unique smell to it too, like rabid death, like goddammit I can't believe I'm still alive, another whiff sniff and snort of glue and I guess it all gets better, and my life ebbs away ... and it's the morning.

It's the morning and I feel so bored. Filled my time with wordless enterprises and now I'm stuck in a relentless turbulence that grips me and spins me and turns me all the way around, and it's the morning and it's the morning, and soon I'll be upside down, and it's the morning. Goddamit it's the morning.

Hurray it's the morning.

Fuck me it's the morning.

I'm so glad the night is over and the morning is here and I can waste my time in the daylight as opposed to the eerie dark of the night and it's the morning it's the morning it's the morning.

Fuck me it's got me again.

Commemorating 50 years in 50 hours

I was thinking if I got pissed off easily, I'd be quite the hypocrite, don't you think? Considering I've made it my vocation to piss off the masses, throw crap into a swirling fan blade and watch as clumps of it splatter the dispersing crowd. See, everybody's been burned by something or someone; me, I've been burned too—by those who crack the whip, clack the ruler against the desk; by those who point and stare, peer-pressuring me to change, to be someone else, something else, to be more like them——he cocks his fist and sends it railing into my eye. My head smacks the pavement, that was me as a kid, persecuted for being different; so in my ripe age I've made it my vocation to offend. Weirdness to an extreme. I recognize that if something you do pisses me off, if I have a problem with you, then it's my problem, because you have the right to do it regardless and I have to sit back and watch it happen—regardlessly.

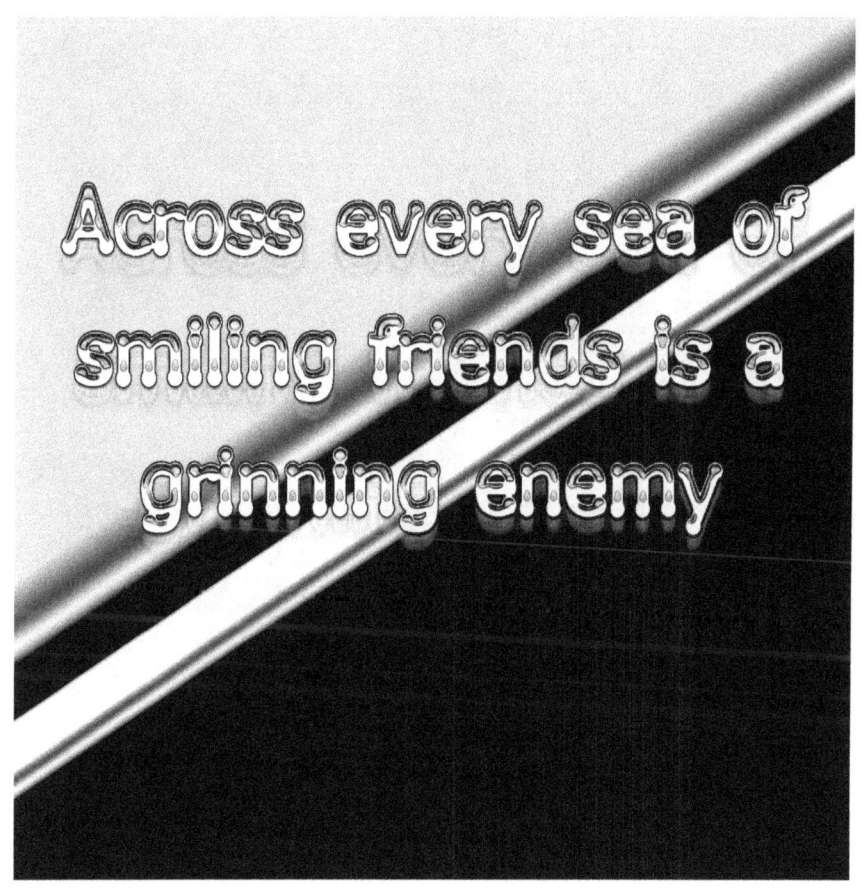

My Own Hell

There are demons in my closet,
skeletons in my backroom,
clawing the walls, and all I can hear
are the sounds of nails scraping wood.
It's maddening, the scratching of ghouls,
tearing slits and crevices in the doors.
The slamming and banging sounds
keeping me awake for endless hours.
It's all so real, so insane,
I lie awake in a straightjacket,
rocking to and fro, praying for it
all to stop, to cease, to end,
but it doesn't ever rest;
maybe it will when I'm dead.
When I'm gone, and I'm riding the waves
straight to Hell.

When I'm surfing fire, a surge of flames,
curling up, recoiling like a whip,
taking me through downtown Hell,
bringing me uptown to where the Devil
sits on Its thrown, waiting to rape me
with a 100-degree rod wrapped in razor-sharp thorns.
I dread it all, the thrashing sounds of my demons
trying to break out, escape and tie me up
with razor-wire which cuts deep into my skin,
as they dance around me like Indians
bopping around a pit of flames.
They wear hellish loincloths, their skin
orange and pockmarked with three green spots
over their noses, which are big like beaks.

I know what they wanna do to me.

Independence Day

Fireworks blast off
it's the Fourth
of July
and fireworks sail
the dark, mysterious sky
of eternity
Every day of the year
people scurry out of their houses
to jobs
punching clocks stacking papers
repeating boring phrases
such as
PAPER OR PLASTIC?
WOULD YOU LIKE FRIES WITH THAT?
DO YOU NEED HELP BRINGING THE BAGS
OUT TO THE CAR?

Every day people shuffle around
in monkey suits playing games
playing putrid fucking GAMES
of life, trying to pretend
playing make-believe.
Waiting—waiting waiting
for sacred salvation/

Tonight flickering flashing lights
sail the heavens and people watch
as their future unfolds
here
now
wasted lives.... boring mundane
wasted life, people dying mundane deaths
It's the Fourth of July and
firework tear up
the dark sky....

TIME

Time to go somewhere, someplace, anywhere, anyplace, everywhere, everyplace; time to be someone, somebody, anyone, anybody, everyone, everybody - - living a lie, a dream, a fantasy, an altered reality - - time to stretch my limits, push and pinch it and watch it dissolve in acidic waste like fire flies fighting and fucking right by my side>>>>>

Some Definition in My Life

I love Punk rock, this is true. I love it more than anything, because it made me, it gave me definition, and definition was always something I lacked growing up in Newton, MA.
THEY had definition, I didn't.
They were football players, I wasn't.
They were baseball players or lacrosse players
they had popularity and girls and money and cars
and I had my rag-tag T-shirt and a FUCK OFF attitude that couldn't be bought, but it was not enough ...
it was never enough until I found Punk rock!

Punk rock spoke to me in ways no girl ever could, it whispered softly in my ear, it spoke to me and promised things ....
it promised something more! something more than what I was getting.... Which was absolutely nooooothing.

Tradition

Tradition is lame.
Let's all get together and do
what our ancestors have done.

Burn witches on the stake.

same mistakes
different day

same mistakes
different day

same mistakes
different day

same mistakes
different day

The Circle Song

The circle spins....
  People hustle
going to their jobs
  as the circle spins.

Their pace stays even,
  Twirling like a top,
it spins and it spins, and
  people go to bed.

The morning sun
  breaks through the clouds.
    Alarm clocks buzzzzzz,
      and eyes begin to budge.

People all around the world
feel groggy as they
get out of bed and hop
into their hot showers.

The circle spins
  like a merry goround,
    it doesn't stop spinning
      until the last man's dead.

——Monotonous
——Dreadful
——Wasteful

People live....
their ugly lives,
working like rats
shuffling papers like monkeys,
      writing reports like mutants.

Like mutant sheep, a monotonous
dreadful wasted thing.

Tick tock—
  the clock is ticking
Tick tock—
  the circle is spinning....

Punch the clock
Monotonous and wretched,
enslaved to the system.
          The human race is doomed.

someday everyone is
going to hate me

WHAT AM I GONNA DO?

WHAT AM I GONNA DO?

WHAT AM I GONNA DO?

A Race to the Top

Like Candy Land
in a forest of
Candy Canes
a tall, windy staircase
remains unscathed.
It's a race to the top.
Ginger Bread Men
& women too
fight to the death
as they climb to the tippity top
of a rickety rocking banister
that popped out of nothing.
One day it was a wasted and dead
plane, the next levels rose straight upward
up up up- to the top
it wound a traversing tapestry of ginger
and frosting and gummy bears
and Mrs. Frosty thought to herself,
How do we exploit this new finding?
Musing over it, a sinister cunt she was,
her nefarious reverie spun a web
of greed and glory and greedy glory.
She masterminded the stakes
and divided the clan into fifty-one states
of rich and tasty candy
and so then the gingerbread men
and Women too
wielding gleaming swords of chocolate
and vanilla spears
and gleaming scythes made of caramel
and shields of cookie dough
lined up at the bottom.
When the hammer dropped in
mounds of creamy icecream
and the peanut flew from inside
the mouth of the sweet and gooey volcano
the men & women of this fantastic world
hurled themselves at the staircase....
... one after another ...

Your fate is dilapidated, a crumbling, destroyed face that clenches up and kisses the damaged demon, the god of blasphemous actions, death and destruction over yonder, and you're shouting, pounding the steel barricades, screaming till your face disintegrates into steaming-hot mounds of pus just bubbling up and dissipating into cloudy crud that your mother and father eat hungrily for supper, they kiss their plastic plates and hurl them, spinning and crashing, into the blood-stained brick oven that explodes when the door snaps closed and the walls crumble, and soon enough you're running, running for your life, running just to die, your arms flailing as your feet, kicking the defeated stadium beneath you, launch you straight into outer space, to never be seen again——because your fate is dilapidated, the end....

I HATE THE SMELL OF PERFUME!

I'm sitting here at this coffee shop, and there is no one anywhere near my general vicinity and suddenly the repugnant smell of perfume breaches my nostrils. I think I know the culprit, though---an old woman more than twenty feet away standing by the counter. What, is she trying to make our noses bleed?

Rappers & Their Bling

Since when are there raging block parties in the ghetto, where half-naked girls dance atop shiny sports cars and mega surround-sound speakers are mounted up on tall stands and hundreds of people are hanging out drinking fucking million-dollar bottles of champagne? And there's a rapper wearing lots and lots of gold—gold teeth, gold rings, a gold necklace, and a fucking wide-rimmed gold clock dangling over his chest—and the music is extremely loud, and nobody in the neighborhood gets mad and complains, nobody who has to work the following day just to eat one lousy meal is screaming out the window, yelling at these rich morons parading around in their million-dollar outfits and saying this is where they grew up. Nobody is telling them to shut the fuck up, you stinkin' posers; I got work in the morning, I'm really poor and I really got work in the morning so I can earn my keep which you clearly don't have to do, judging from the flashy hubcaps glimmering beneath your lowriders; so please, *please* shut the fuck up and go back to your rich suburban homes and let me sleep in peace. Go back to Malibu, goddammit; back to Beverly Hills, or wherever it is that breeds you stupid fucking posers——and this old woman who has her hair in curls is waving a rolling pin out the window scolding these turds that don't belong here in the first place; she calls them wannabes one last time and slams the window shut with an angry thump.

Tell me where this exists! Please! I really wanna know! And if you do, I promise I won't laugh at you and ask if you're on crack. I won't! I promise!

if you want to
love me

don't half-ass it

Point & Click

I wish my writing would incite a riot

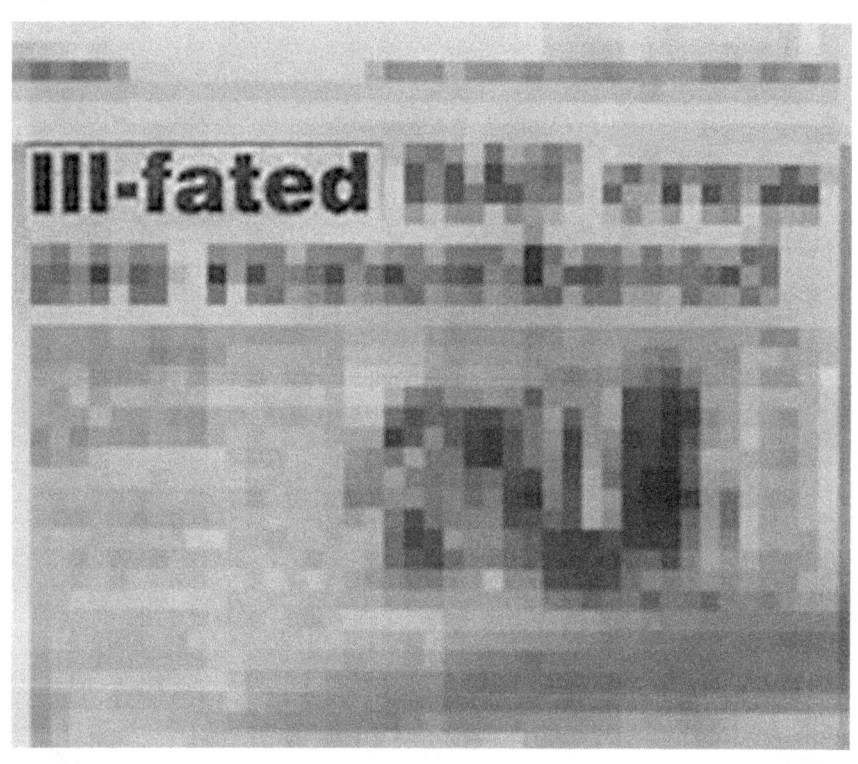

What's the difference between crazy and unconventional?

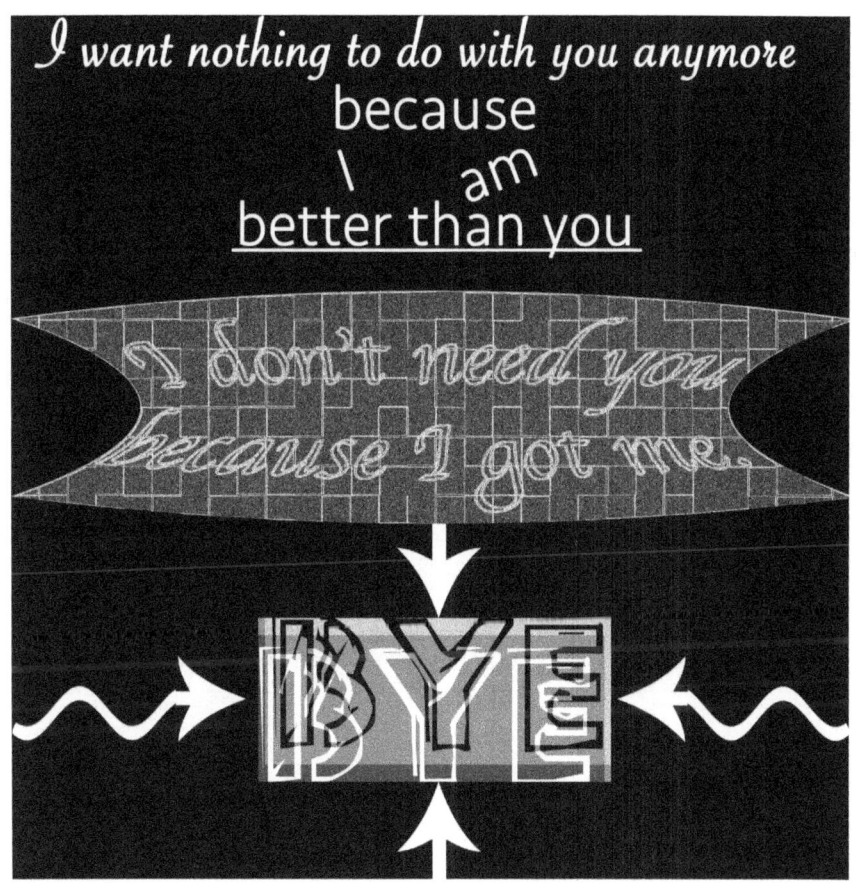

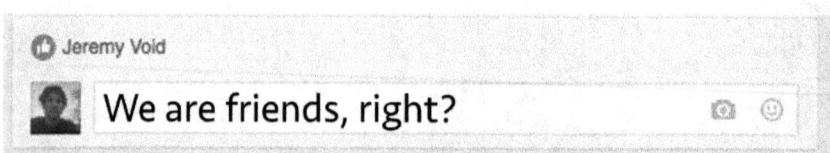

a new poem

a new poem on a night i have nothing to say—what shud i say? a new poem is such a fright when the words dont come as naturally as before. ohmygod, theyre jus not flowing//// i wanna write something now but i cant i cant i cant & this fact is killing me, sir. a new poem is deadly when it doesnt pour out of your brain like chicken noodle soup. gut pudding—yum yum yum. maybe im hungry or im craving caffein. or something to set my mind alight & something to ease the block thats stabbing into my brain right now.

why wont somebody kill me please.

Grow Up   Act Your Age

Two Phrases I Never Really Cared for When I Was a Kid

All That Time when people barked jeremy when are you gonna grow up I **Was** Acting My Age. Just the Thing Is, They Were All Just in Too Much a Rush to Grow Up Themselves, on the run from their own ages. but you see, for me, I Didn't Care Too Much about What Others Thought or Felt and Feeling That Way Was Quite Disinhibiting, as if i had inhibitions to begin with, which i didn't. i was satisfied with my own immaturity, i was fine with being a Kid for a few more years, because growing up and holding down the same job day in, day out seemed quite the boring life and I Wanted None of It

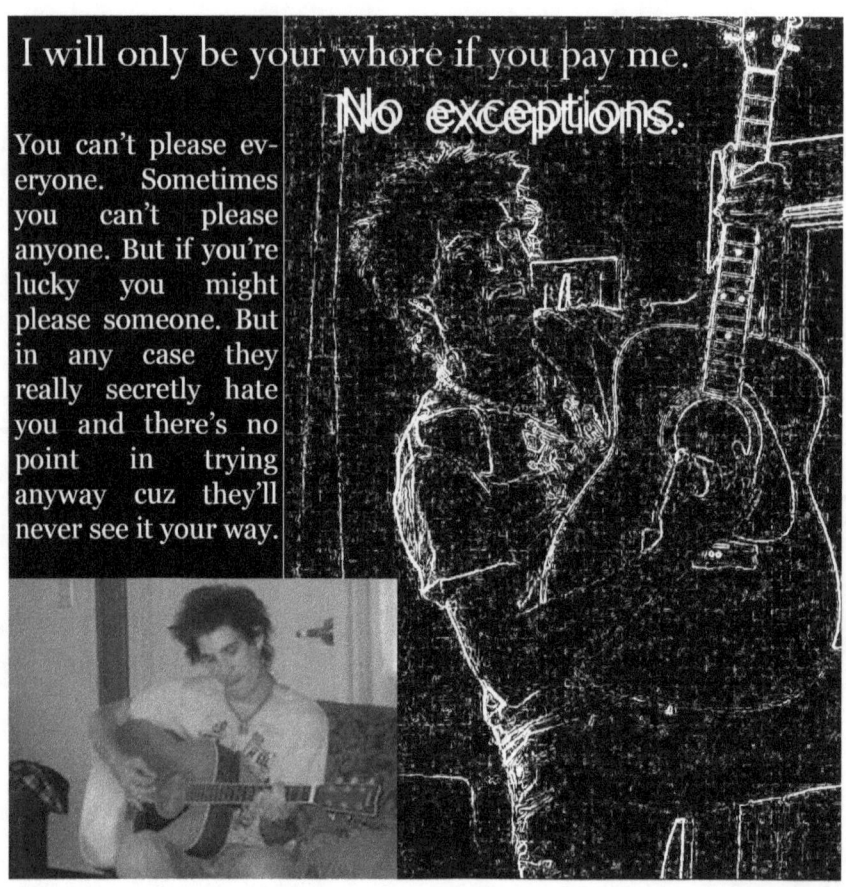

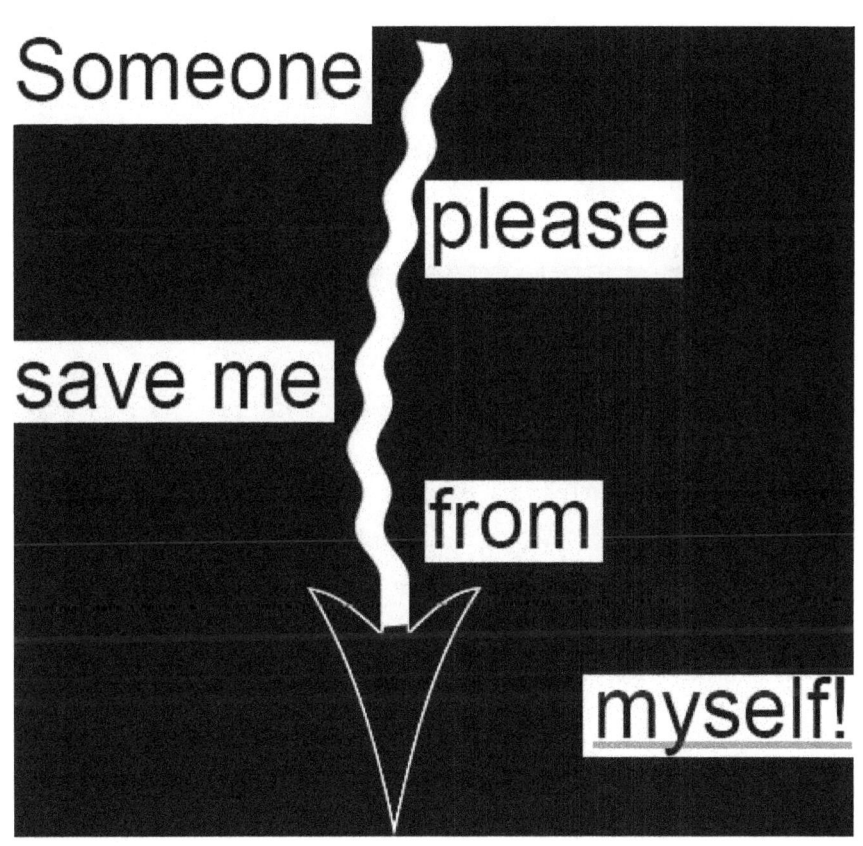

Can't Take the STRAIN

We've all got our problems
Everyone Is Number One

Standing in a crowded room
in a packed stadium

faces like numbers
haunt you till the day
that you die

We've all got our problems
Everyone Is Number One

when i raise my fist to the sky,
you better drop dead.
when i shout at the moon,
you better gimme all your money.
when i run, stomp, stagger, & spit,
you better leave me the fuck alone because
a knife is an ugly protrusion when its
jutting out of your back, all bloodied & gross.

FUCK THIS

I'm not a fucking pet. I'm a human being and I got feelings. I'm not gonna be tethered to a girl I got feelings for who just wants to be my fucking friend cuz I'm not her "type." First of all, there's the obvious: in order to fit a type I have to be put inside a box, and I'm not inside **A BOX**. Which means I can't be anyone's type. And second of all, I just met this chick, and I don't care enough about her to follow her around all day like a fucking puppy dog in hopes for something that ain't ever gonna happen. Frankly I got better fucking things to do.

So there!

waiting for the drugs to kick in
this drug called life
they say it will kick in eventually—
——but when??

> Forgive me for not being excited about sitting and watching paint dry.

That's terrible,
boring crap that
makes my eyes bleed
when I see it.
It's so bad that
my dick leaks pus
from experiencing it.
Shite, shite, shite!

<u>Or maybe that's a good thing.</u>

Maybe your goal is to make
me hate you.
In which case you'd be a success.
Now, wouldn't you?

What You See Is What You Get, only what you see is a liar and a deceiver who will cut you down so fast your head will spin.

Everyone I know is joining hands in a magical death dance down the center of awestruck faces & flashing lights. Me, I avoid the lights & step out into the night. The night doesn't flash me except with entrancing wisdom that only the social elite possess, from a lifetime of cars doing donuts around planet earth. Stay strange, stranger than whacky America with its unification, with its coporate conformity—& yet I find myself quite depressed cuz I don't seem to fit into their plan—the power of suggestion, the hour of death. When everyone I know is falling neatly in line like cattle, where do I go? I'm dying from irony, it's a twisted joke & I'm the punchline. I say defy everyone, defy the system, defy God while you're at it, cuz he's the one who created this "master plan" in the first place. Go against the flow or you'll lose yourself to a faux-existence. The Thought Police? No need. They got a dresscode & if you don't submit, your peers will turn against you. I run away, I avoid confrontation, I do everything in my power——but what power?? My peers got the whip, just another victim of inculcation—again & again, I've got a choice. Voices like thunder, left-wing hudu tying me up in chains. The power of suggestion, the hour of death. Peer pressure tearing me up, & soon I'll get married.

the end

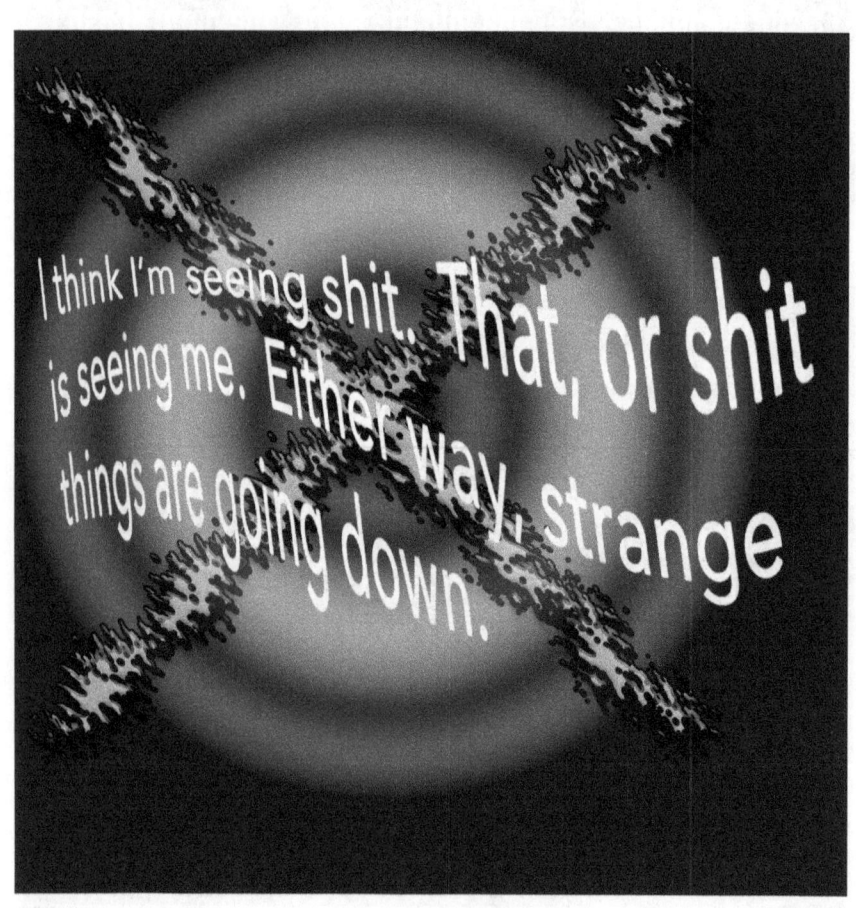

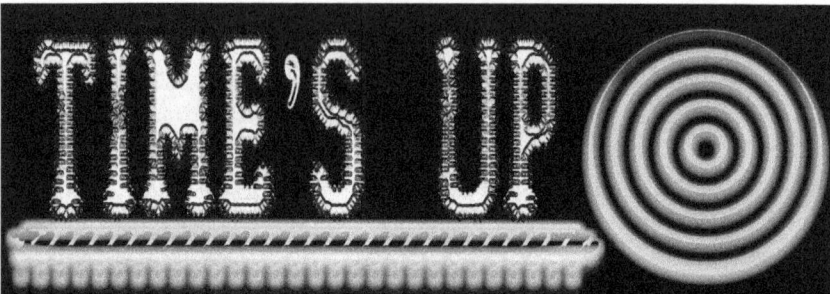

TIME'S UP

I'm spent. The day's up. I'm lost and wound up. I'm looking. I punch the clock——tick tick tock, a senseless rattle. I'm jittery and annoyed, tired and so damn self-absorbed. I'm lost and I just don't know. I watch the clock————the second hand jumps, and I jump; the minute hand flinches, and I flinch. When will my time be up?? It's a relentless cycle, senseless and so damn psychotic. I watch the clock the hour hand winks at me, sweat stings my eyes. I'm waiting, I'm waiting, I'm waiting waiting waiting...

The second hand jumps, and i jump. It's just not enough, not enough not enough ... the minute hand flinches, and I ... I ... I tear open the drawer, shuffle through pieces of scrap paper, grab the gun. It feels nice in my grip, like pure fucking power. Just squeeze the trigger and see where it gets you. I stick it against my head....

The hour hand winks at me, and fuck you time—I pull....

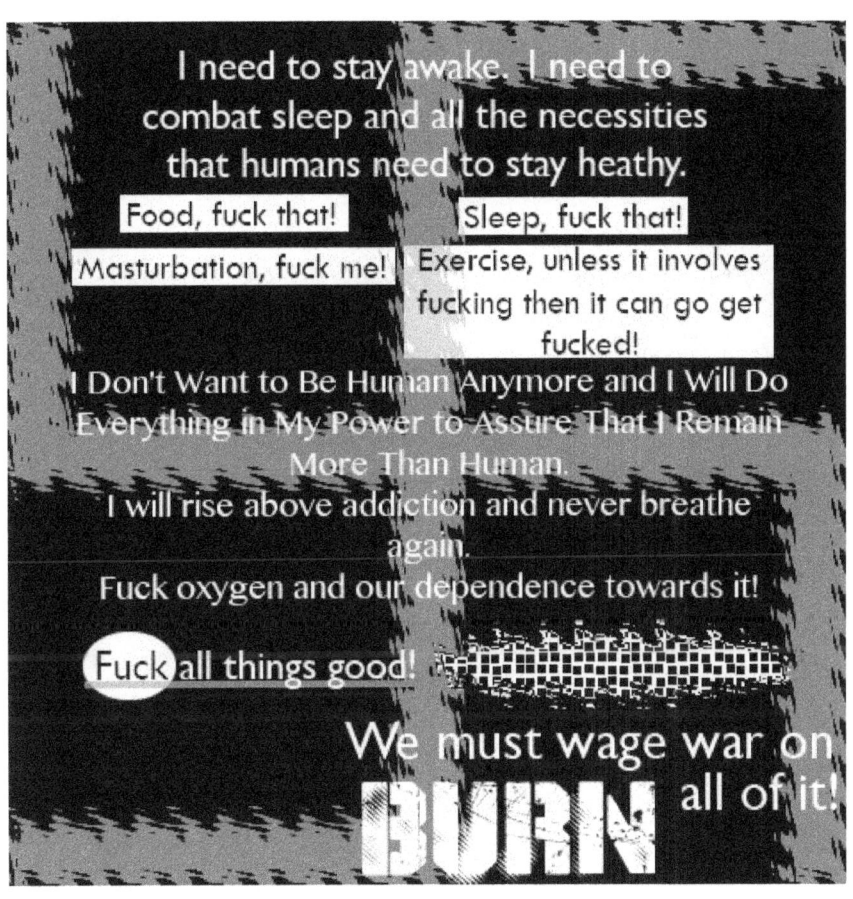

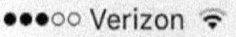 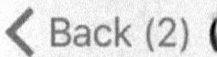 

> Why do I gotta act like such a fucking idiot all the time??

> Why do I gotta act like such a fucking idiot all the time??

> Why do I gotta act like such a fucking idiot all the time??

> Why do I gotta act like such a fucking idiot all the time??

> Why do I gotta act like such a fucking idiot all the time??

Read 6:49 AM

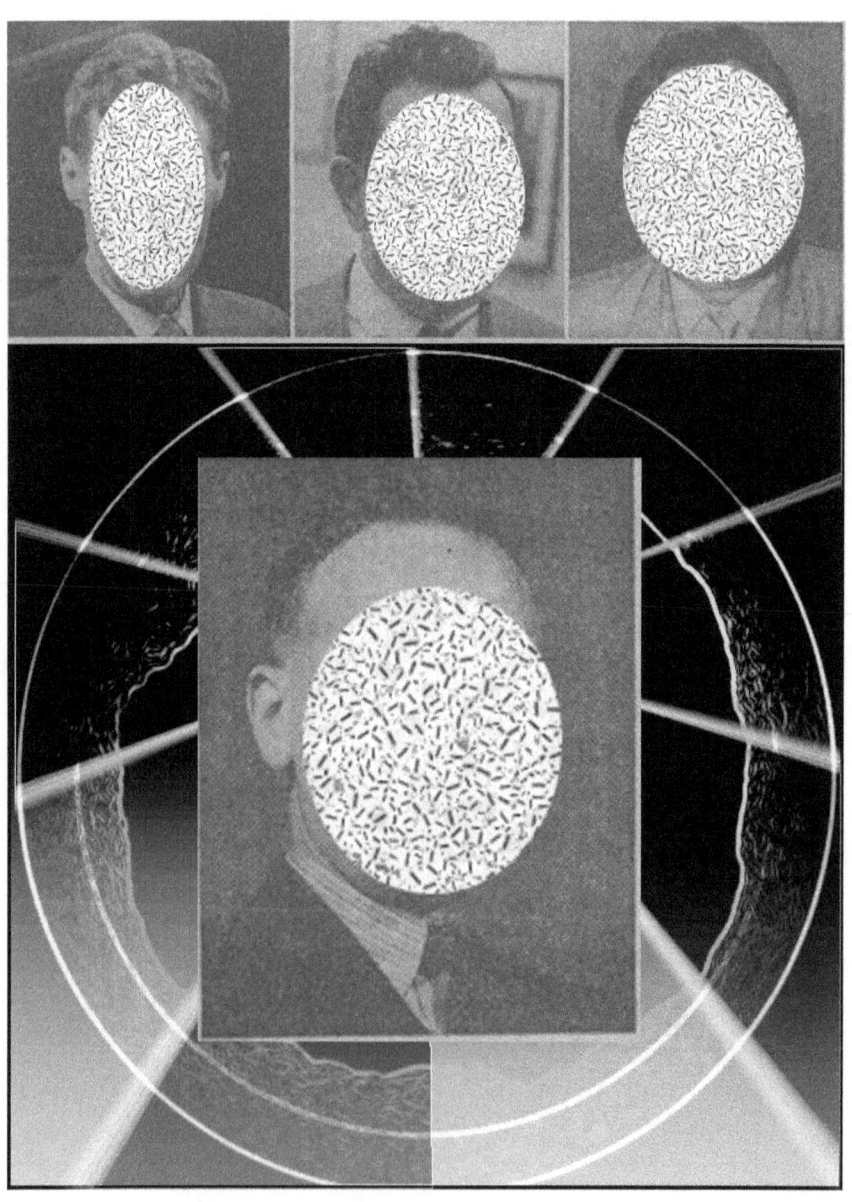

Fuckin bullshit is what it is. You see pictures of people dressed all in Punk costumes—because costumes are all they are—hanging out with others in the same scummy outfits, but then you click next, and the next picture to appear on your screen is of that same Punk out clubbing with cunts in baggy pants and name-brand T-shirts with strobe lights flickering in the backgrounds, all dancing as if to hip hop or whatever fuckin music these college kids are into today, and it makes me fuckin sick, makes me want to spew and slash. I never heard of a grey-area Punk, those who are half-Punk and half-something else, or maybe a third Punk, a third of this, and a third of that.

Point & Click

Right now my thoughts are firing with Gatling gun velocity. My mind an explosion of insight, but don't ask me what that insight entails, because I may very well get lost in a tangent about what an arm pit looks like when there's a baboon sitting on your back and a Pikachu—yes, a real life Pikachu—eating out of your butt.

i am goin to do somethin stupid, it's how i get my kix

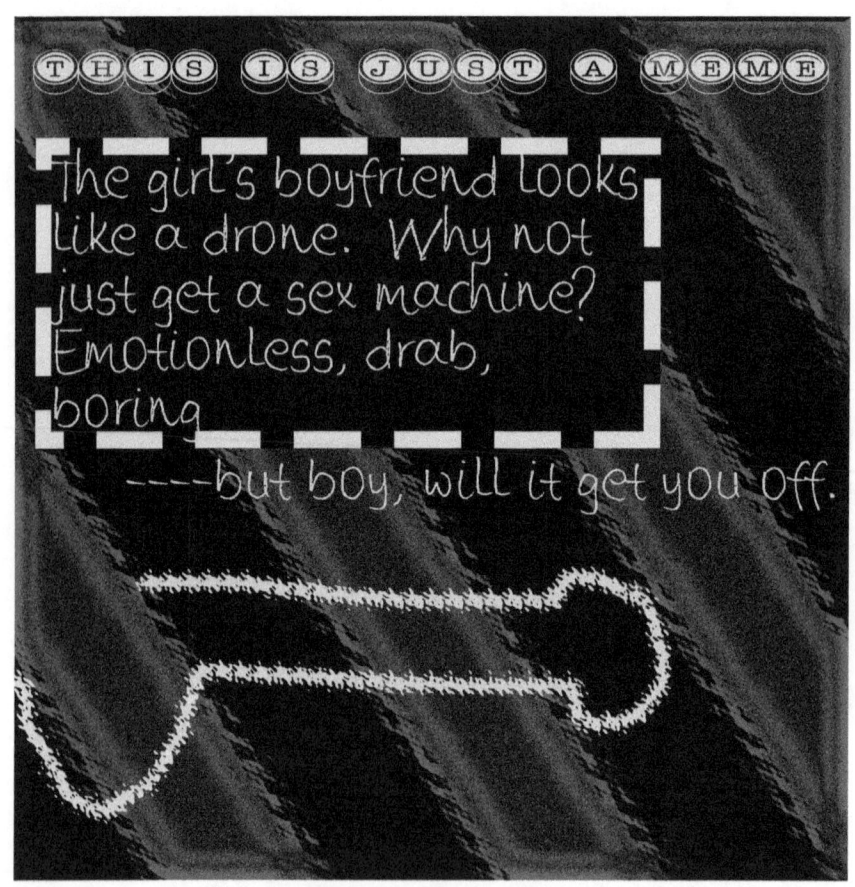

I won't remember you when I'm famous

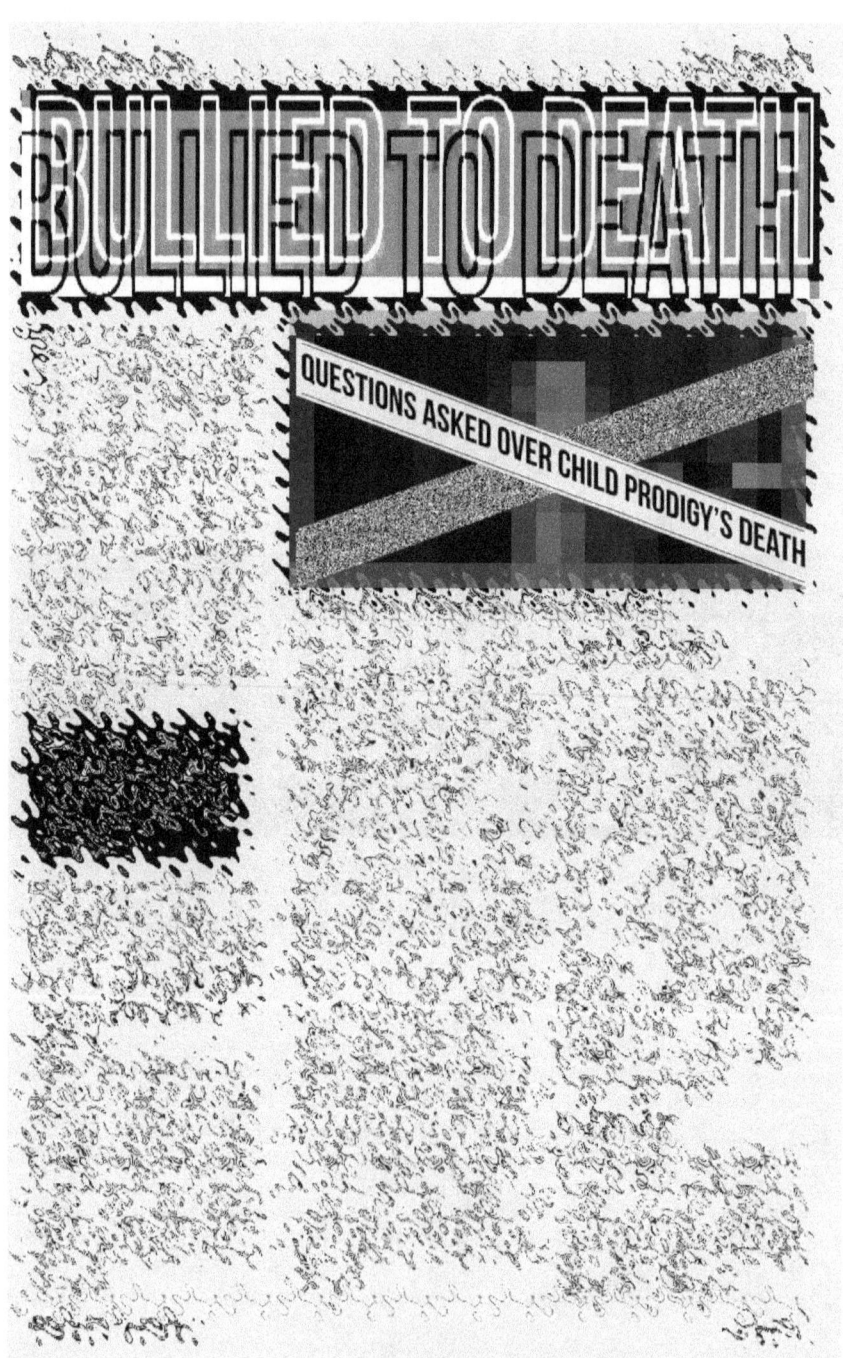

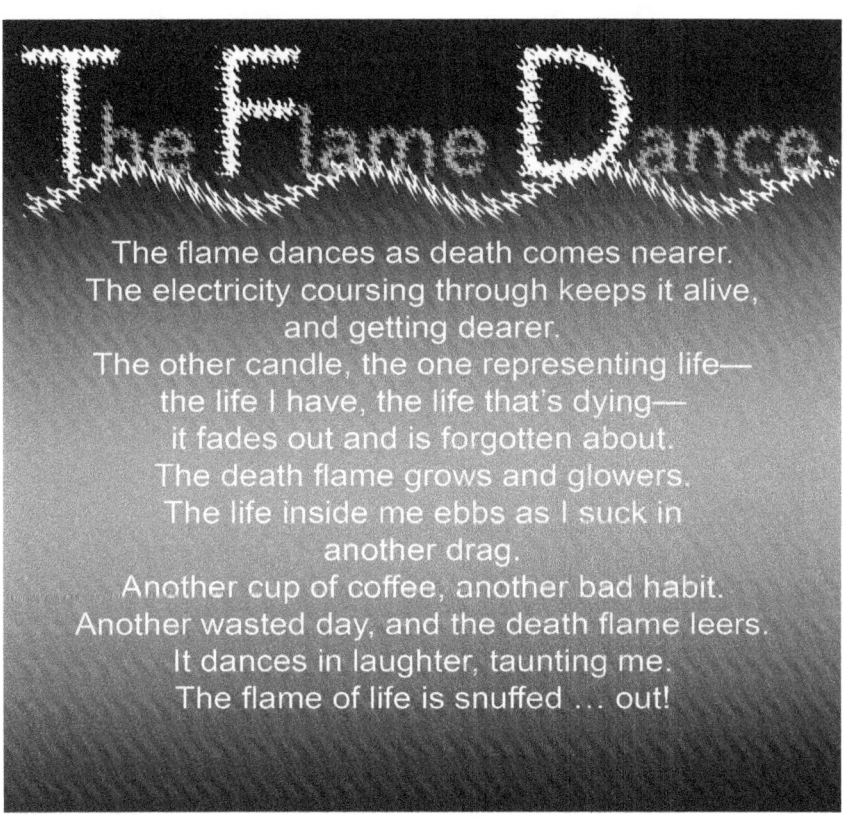

The Flame Dance

The flame dances as death comes nearer.
The electricity coursing through keeps it alive,
and getting dearer.
The other candle, the one representing life—
the life I have, the life that's dying—
it fades out and is forgotten about.
The death flame grows and glowers.
The life inside me ebbs as I suck in
another drag.
Another cup of coffee, another bad habit.
Another wasted day, and the death flame leers.
It dances in laughter, taunting me.
The flame of life is snuffed ... out!

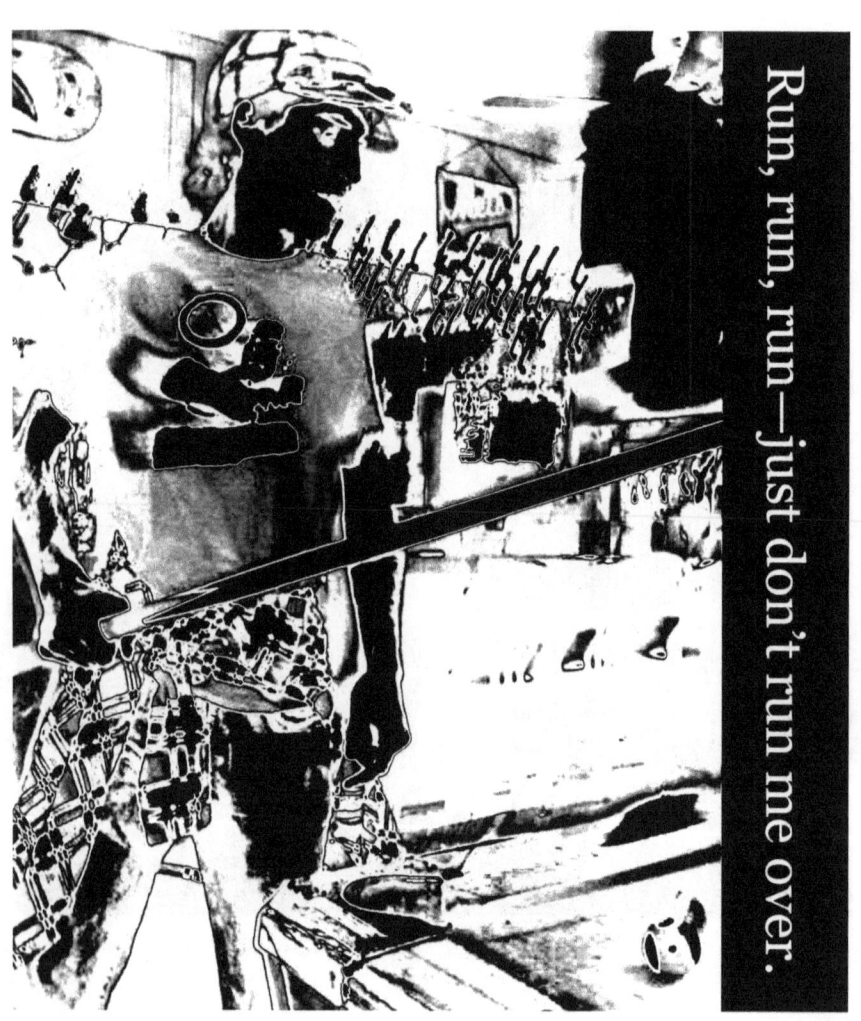

At some point I will piss everyone off. I don't want to piss anyone off. But today I will piss someone off. What I do want is to climb into your head and, uh ... fuck it, just fuck your mind, fill it with gruesome logic that is sure to break your heart. But I don't want you to hate me. On the contrary, I want you to love me, hold me up on the pedestal and then spit in my face. I know I'm mixed up, I know I'm demented, I know I got nothing realistic to say about anything, I know everything that you know and more and yet I feel like I know nothing about that, nothing about anything and in the end it's all the same to me. So there.

I feel like that needed to be said.

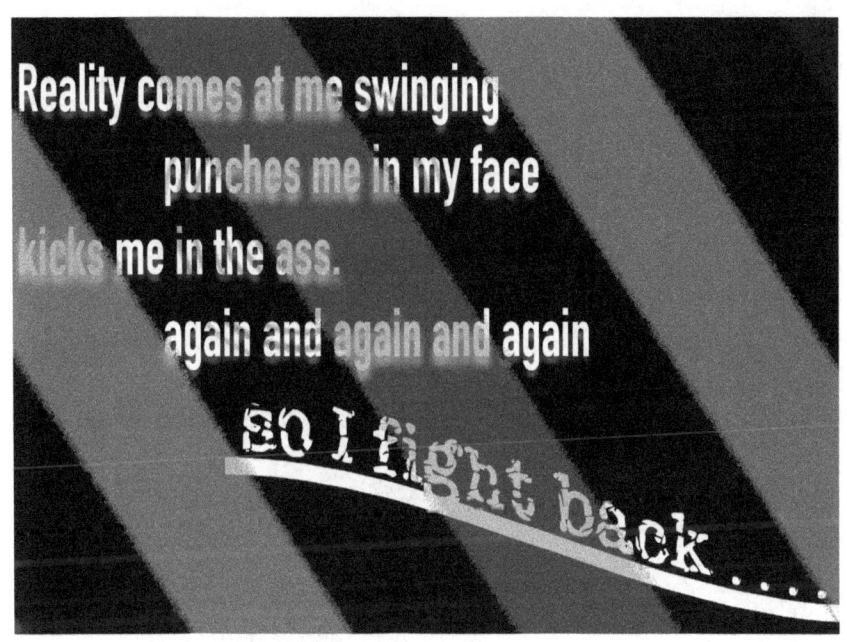

True Romance

Lost in your glare
your smile is the only reason
that I'm here
the glint of your shiny white teeth
and your hair that waves majestic
lines through the air.

I'm lost and I'm alone and the only thing
that could make this moment better

is if you noticed me too....

So I kiss the mystery on the lips
and drift away on that sullen fantasy
of what could be
of me and you

if only you would notice me too.

Stalemate

When you read something by someone you absolutely despise
and the words bring actual tears to your eyes
and you hate yourself for that fact,
but you can't help it, it's just too damn sad
and for once you understand
For Once you understand what it's like to live in said person's sad sad life ...
and suddenly you feel a connection that you could have never imagined feeing before
and there you go: You've gotten over your self-righteousness because you realized he is no different than you, you are no different than him, you're both just another fuckin victim of this society's fucked-up condition....

Waiting waiting, boring boring, nothing's new, I'm sick and bored and I'm sitting, snoring, and wasting my time fingering the hole I cut in my enemy's throat. You know what I'm saying? Cuz I sure don't. I'm choking on life as life chokes me up, I'm banging the walls and kicking the ceiling as the walls and the ceiling close in on me. I'm losing a battle that was never meant to be fought, and people they say to just keep my head up and play it straight, but I'm too crooked to play any games they lay out before me, cuz the Pawns are busted and the Rooks have run away, and the Knights are looking at me, and suddenly this aint life, this is just a game, it's just a game, a game, but they gave it a name and its name is Life and I'm riding in a plastic car with my plastic wife past plastic houses and this is LIFE, and I think I might be turning plastic myself, becoming a pawn to be maneuvered at the will of my masters and it's all assbackwards but I seem to be trapped here. It's just a game they told me; and I believed them too.

You say you believe in total freedom, until I say something out of line. I tell you you don't need to apologize to me ever because nothing you say or do matters in the end. But when I speak my own mind I suddenly become the bad guy. I suddenly become the enemy when all I did was voice my concerns, I was confused I was confused I was confused, and you say I shouldn't have been, don't contact me again. The end. I gave you more than enough slack in every facet of our co-existence, but I never got any back and now I'm sad, I feel deceived, I'm wondering what did I do that was so bad, other than say I was confused I was confused I was confused, which I guess forced you to choose and you chose to leave....

                                            Goodbye.

Either too smart, or too stupid, I just can't decide. One way or another, I'm too young to do it. Fuck me, I blew it!

Last night I got a free pink button-down shirt in Burlington, VT. This guy says to me, "Can i bum a smoke?" and I reply, "Can I have your shirt?" He thinks for a moment, then shrugs and starts unbuttoning his shirt down to his half-tattooed pale and somewhat bloated stomach, and hands it to me. It was a nice shirt, although it was pink, although it was ripped, which cancelled out the fact that it was clearly the kind of shirt a yo-yo would wear; so I felt somewhat bad and handed him two cigarettes instead of one, and he walked away smiling and shirtless and I walked to the store holding a brand-new pink button-down shirt that cost me only two cigarettes. So I guess then it wasn't entirely free.

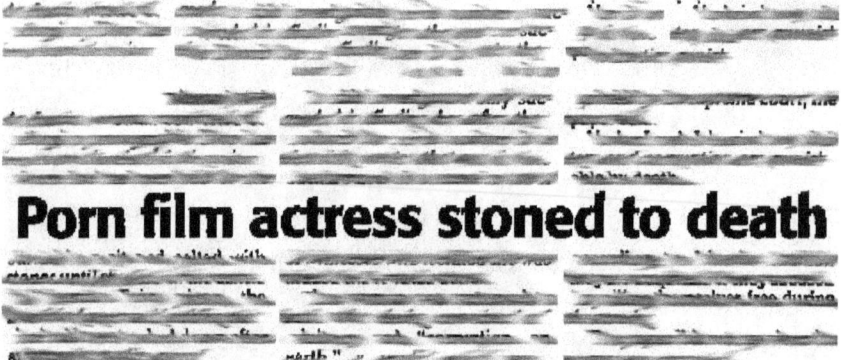

Crown of Thorns

It was a time when
nothing made sense.
I thought the world
was coming to an end/
Live your life like
you're already dead,
    is what I said,
        and I suffered
           the consequences
              of a nowhere existence.
    I suffered at the brunt of
a life lost and non-existent.
I was out to lunch,
        said my friends.

Everywhere I went,
it was all the same.
A hysterical descent
that drove me insane.
I lived fast only to
be knocked to my knees.
I crawled on all fours
I pleaded and I screamed/
        but for what??
It was all just a dream>/>/>/>/

Dear Penis

Please release me from your clutches

Thank You
Jeremy Void

I am such a hypocrite and I feel this strong, overbearing urge to justify my ignorance by saying, Hey, everyone's a hypocrite, we're all the same in the end, just useless vessels living in a delusional state, and at least I have the guts to own my own hypocrisy, right? I mean, the bad hypocrites—since we're all hypocrites in the end, as I have said, there must be degrees of hypocrisy so that I'm not so bad after all, not so full of shit, not as much of a sanctimonious bastard as the rest of America's wasted inhabitants—the bad hypocrites are the ones who won't fess up to their bullshit, you know the kind. Noses angled upward, always ready to point out your flaws at any given moment, almost as if they carry around a list of defects and description and if anyone so much as acts out any of the follies on their list, an extended index finger drops like the judge's mallet, racking an invisible podium as they point out what's wrong with you—those are the worst: so self-righteous, so anal-retentive, so snobby and vindictive—those are definitely the worst breed of humans to ever inhabit planet earth. And I sure ain't that bad, am I? Like, I mean, sometimes I find myself preaching on a subject that I know nothing about, preaching like my word is gospel, with an unyielding desire to show other like-minded individuals what I wrote, as opposed to standing out like a Muslim in Texas, a sore thumb as you will, like a wretched case of herpes that had spread beyond the boundaries of my mouth, having dominated my entire face in a grotesque mask of bubbly puss and bloody zit-like bumps that radiate and pop. See, I admire anyone who has the guts to stand against the mob. Every recognizable revolutionary to have stepped foot on this planet stood against the mass majority in some way or another, and I think that's great, and I promote such action in my writing, telling others to step forth on angry feet with a righteous clenched fist reaching for the sky—as long as you recognize that your newfound feeling of rectitude is founded in bullshit you'll be okay—and I think all should stand for something, but what do I stand for but nothing? I write politically driven poems and share em with like-minded folk, and what does that do in the way of revolution? This one time, years ago, I sat on the curb eating pizza out of a box and when I had eaten every last bit of it I tossed the box on the ground and this guy pulled up in his car and asked me who's gonna pick that up?—and I just looked at him and shrugged saying, Um, not me, and walked away. So I guess we're all hypocrites, huh? only some of us are sicker than others and the sickest are the ones who stand for causes so righteously that everyone who opposes them is wrong—so glad I'm not one of those!

We are all cunts
to a nation of even bigger
cunts.
We are all lost.....

I think I'm gonna start a political party called the Anti-Trendies

Anyone who joins is a poser

Nothing to Say

Nothing to Do

Nothing to Say

Nothing to Do

Can't decide
whether I'm dead or alive.
Too much pressure
daydreaming of suicide.
Gotta relax
put on some tunes.
If I don't see you soon
I might just blow a fuse.

This is life
a de-existing track
I'm bored and fed up
nobody's got my back.
This is life they tell me/
This is death they avoid....
This is living. Right!
I'm dying in this tremoring void.

Point & Click

It seems to be a common misconception that immaturity means constantly seeking pleasure, instant gratification, on a never-ending quest for fun, it becomes all about me and what I want and I'll throw a tantrum if you don't give it to me now; whereas maturity is just the opposite, where it becomes all about everyone else, get a job, get married, have kids, calm down, slow down, you're getting older and you can no longer maintain that fast-paced lifestyle anymore, become a slave to the system, too jaded to enjoy life, just brood and work and brood and work, go down to the pub and get drunk hating your mere existence while your fellow coworkers do the same— is that what anyone wants?

But on the contrary, immaturity is either seeking pleasure 24-7 OR never seeking pleasure again because you've got a job to keep. Maturity, on the other hand, is recognizing when it is okay for one to goof off and when one must step up and do the right thing, work hard play hard, as you will. So when you see me in downtown Rutland goofing on all the stuck-up, jaded shoppers who mosey past me with a rotten chip on their shoulder, a demented monkey treating their backs like a set of bongo drums, don't tell me to grow up, act my age, you're 28-years old for godsake so when are you gonna act like it?

When are you gonna be revived from the dead? Rise from your tormented coma of jaded waste, a boring vessel on this planet to serve this system which breeds concepts that this is what it means to be a HUMAN BEING. I know when to care about others, I may be a goofball a clown a laughing lowlife but when life beats you down I'll be the first one to hold out my hand and lift you back up. Don't tell me I'm immature because I'm living my life and you are not, on the run from a child that's hidden in the darkest region of your forgotten soul, a child caged and praying that one day this "man" this "adult" this "civilized human being" will lighten up and let it run free like it was meant to be. Maturity has nothing to do with how one acts, it has to do solely on how one understands and conceptualizes actions and reactions, having a greater knowledge about oneself, that's all there is to say about it....

I am in Boston performing Lethal Erection to a filth-ridden sea of testosterone and hormones as the crowd nods off with visions of sado-masochism and they all hop and slash, delving deeper and deeper into their own private wet dreams.

only you can start forest fires
where are the gas tanks? let's burn this motherfucker to the GROUND

Vindictive Arrogance

One moment I'm determined to tear everyone down, the next moment I'm concerned I might have torn someone down.

One moment I'm brutally blunt, the next moment I'm brutally second-guessing my previous transgressions.

Was it something that I said?
Truly, I meant you no harm.

I can assure you my arrogant and cocky demeanor are only as a result of an overall dissatisfaction with self——give myself a moment to cool off and reflect, boy I might stake my head to the ground, slug me in the eye socket with a long, steel club with a nail jutting out the top.

Everyone hates me—well fuck em anyway.
Everyone hates me—I feel guilty and ashamed
borderline psychotic, bold and indecisive, a prick with a conscious—see that's me.

And I'm proud

And I'm self-loathing

And I'm sure
but so unsure that I might seem like a different person.

Don't need to worry about me being two-faced, either
because I'm only two-faced to those I don't like>>>>
and yet I don't like anyone;;;;;
so you see, I'm in a bit of a bind ...

But please like me, it's free of charge
just please let me into your heart

so I can tear you up from the inside
that's all I really want in the end................

Indecisions

I was just thinking. See, I never seem to be sure of anything when talking to you in person so I always feel the need to share a poem or a rant or a prose poem or something anything whatever when conversing about deep, intellectual topics. I realize (and had this pointed out to me recently so it's still fresh in my mind)) that often when conversing with others I change my mind on certain topics, like I'm trying to impress others by giving my thoughts first hearing what they have to say then changing my opinion to fit that of said person with whom I am currently conversing. That's partially true, see; but for the most part the second answer is usually the most honest one, it's like I don't know how to put it unless in solitude with nothing but my own thoughts a pen and a piece of paper, so giving a half-assed response at first is the best I can do in the moment and then when said person puts it in a way that I can relate to and/or agree with, I say Yeah that's about right— —what he said>>> So it may seem to others that I waited for their response for their answer before I could be sure of my own opinion before I could relay how I "actually" feel on the subject, like I need their approval to think—like I'm afraid if I spoke true they might REJECT me—but that's not the issue, and no one would understand unless they walk a day in my shoes, see. And then I'll need to show said person a poem I wrote in support of their argument just so they know how I feel, and just so I have a knack for words and descriptions, philosophically driven in the privacy of my own personal hell, sitting at home at a coffee shop in the back of a restaurant jotting down notes and words and sentences in my beat-up notebook like a madd poet, see....
....Like the madd poet that I am.
I was thinking of this issue because of what went on moments ago when I sat in the back of the coffee shop on the comfortable couch (but not so comfortable that I could fall asleep and dream sleazy fantasies surrounded by yuppies wondering what's with this strange, rough-up man snoozing and nodding off in the back of the shop with a book in his lap and a pen in his hand) editing the new *Smash a Lightbulb: Poetry for Lowlifes* when an older couple (and I mean OLD) sitting on the couch across from me looked over and the fat dude sitting to the left of the old (but still kind of attractive, as old women go) woman said that he applauded me for reading and turned to his wife/girlfriend/just friend or maybe even his fuck-buddy for all I know and asked her when do you ever see someone these days reading a book, let alone a book arched from use with pages bent and slightly torn, and this led to a brief conversation about what screens do to our culture, and before he spoke his opinion on the subject I said Yeah screen are terrible, brutally destroying attention spans everywhere... but there are the perks I guess. He said curtly What perks? screen are all bad.... Yeah you're right, I agreed, they pretty much are. Do you see what I mean? So while he and this woman of unknown classification and origin took a gander at some of my own books that I had on hand, we talked about the detrimental affect screens have on our youth on our culture how they're destroying our minds (as I type this piece on my laptop in the same spot in the back of the coffee shop I'm such a hypocrite), and all the time I wanted to show him the poem "On the Edge of Madness" I wrote last night that supports these claims and makes the claims very beautifully poetically if I might say so myself....

Anyway, my ride's here I've gotta go.

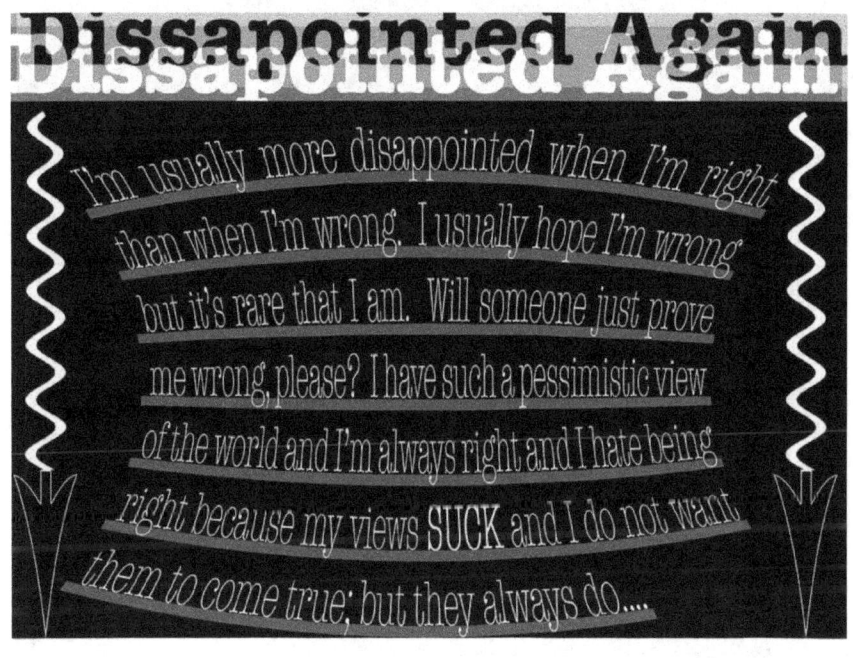

Cursed

Being intelligent and introspective and possessing the ability to remember everything that happens to you is a curse. She says she didn't keep the fact that she has a fiancé a secret. She would refer to these people as "My People" and when I asked her who's that? she'd say her kid and then mumble a name under her breath. I thought nothing of the mumbled name (because if she doesn't choose to annunciate, then it must not be important anyway, right?), which turns out is her finance's name. She tells me she'll get over her crush on me—what the fuck! So she admits there were sparks which implies that she did keep it a secret from me. And the worst part is, I knew this would happen. I knew the moment I called her out on it she'd turn on me, which implies that I'm absolutely right about everything and she just doesn't want to face it. I'm cursed, I'm telling you.

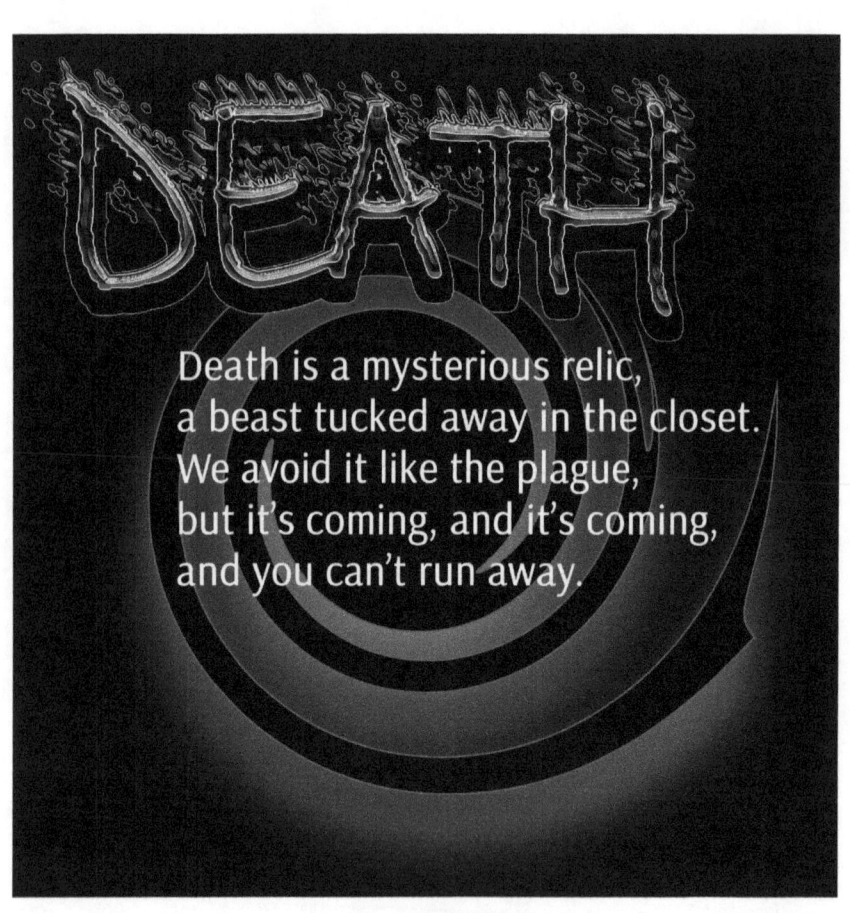

THE ART WORLD

The other day I went on bandcamp.com in search of more bands that I might be into. See, I listen to a very specific type of music. I listen to '77 Punk, or '77-style Punk for bands to have hatched in a later generation. It's called '77 Punk because of two bands, really—two bands I'm not really into myself. In 1977 came the first edition of Punk magazine in New York City, with the Ramones on the front cover, and then overseas came the Sex Pistols who put Punk rock on the map with their infamous manager Malcolm McLaren who pulled off the Great Rock and Roll Swindle it was called, even though Punk rock was already around since the late '60s, early '70s. So it's called '77 Punk.

I went on bandcamp.com with the attempt to find more similar-sounding bands that have come from a more modern era, loud, fast, catchy, and energetic, with a crass melody that will singe your ears if not careful. So the first thing I did was a general search of the genre "Punk Rock."

200 bands

200 bands self-categorized as "Punk rock." Not that any of them are any less Punk than any other, which they aren't I realize. But to my well-trained ears I couldn't find what I was looking for. I browsed through at least a dozen bands before giving up on my search and resorting back to the bands I'm most familiar with.

See, that's the problem. In a day & age where everyone has an equal means to produce their own batch of crap, the good art gets lost in the shuffle. When everyone has the ability to be an artist, everyone will be an artist and therefore no one is an artist.

When everyone is an artist, no one is an artist.

Like Hitler had the idea to fly over England and drop boxes over Euros all across the land, because that in effect would crash the economy. When there's an unlimited amount of money at our disposal, the dollar becomes worthless.

So this is the state of the art world. So how do people cope with it in this state? Who has the most followers. Who is the most liked by the masses. But there lies another problem: If four people have three followers each, and one person looms over them with a total of ten followers, then who should I follow? Hmm, let's see. The one with ten followers looks more promising. So now there are four people with three followers each and one person looms over them with a total of eleven followers. The rich get richer and the poor get poorer—the popular gets more popular and the less popular gets even less popular.

See, this is the problem I'm exhibiting>>> I'm not a likable or social person and those who are more likeable and social, with a bigger pair of tits and a brighter set of teeth that shine invitingly in all the pictures, are sucking up LIKEs like a sponge, whereas I'm draining LIKEs like a VOID.

I guess I'm just destined to fail....

Gotta Love Those Mannequins, cuz we live in a mannequin nation, a plastic reality, with made-up faces and phony fragrances....

People spend their whole lives applying makeup to their faces, covering up their zits and warts, and then they have the nerve to make fun of someone who can't afford to use makeup in more ways than one. It makes them feel better about themselves. But in the end we're all the same: we're all sick and trying to make a place for ourselves in a sadistic world run by giants who wouldn't think twice about stomping our faces into dirt.

Bored & Frustrated

The bomb is set to go off.
It's set to disrupt.
The toxicity is billowing up in
the city.... This wretched piece of wasteland
the anxiety the boredom the pent-up hate
capped up & ignored, thrown in the backseat
of your minivan, the walls undulating as it
overflows with rage—— Aaaaaaaaaaahhh!!!

I'm sick   & demented
Take it or leave it
  but won't you take me with you/
Join me why won't you
  Join me as I   disintegrate/
Plummet with me
I'm vulnerable   & lost
falling into your arms
  catch me
  kick me
  but please don't forget me
  as you direct me   away   from   you/

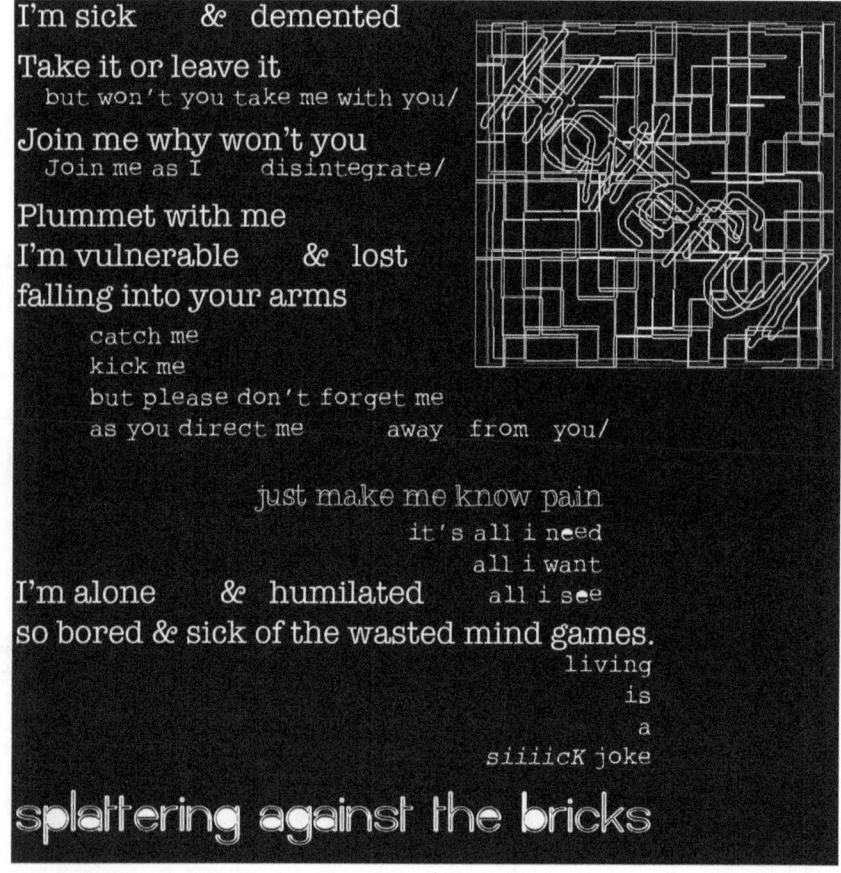

    just make me know pain
     it's all i need
     all i want
I'm alone   & humilated   all i see
so bored & sick of the wasted mind games.
     living
     is
     a
    siiiicK joke

splattering against the bricks

Into the Madness

another night
another dream
another fright
ANOTHER scream

I delve into the madness,
thumbing through it as I pick which
deranged emotion I would feel
today———the morning is immense
the daylight breaching the sky
and I crawl back into my pillow
hoping for relief.

The day begins with a start.
I feel shaken and distraught, already
dreaming up a diabolical scheme to
partake in this evening.
Maybe spraypaint my name across
the sun and watch my fellow man
perish as it disintegrates.

The morning sometimes
makes me feel alive.
But mostly I feel deader than dead
———so dead
I feel kinda high and you know,
I never wanna die although I know
the inevitable is only
seconds away. Its ticking & ticking
as it gains momentum and will soon wash over me.

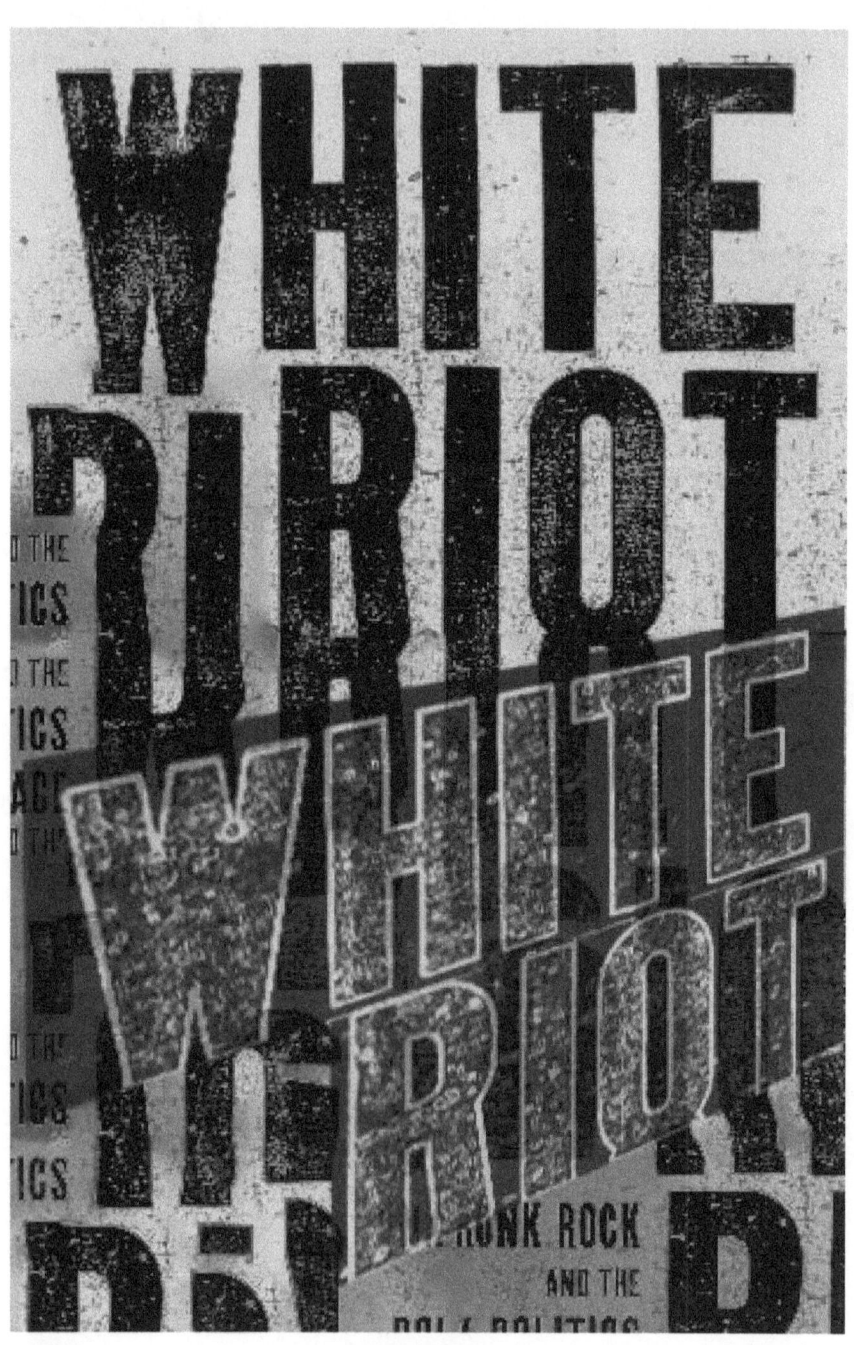

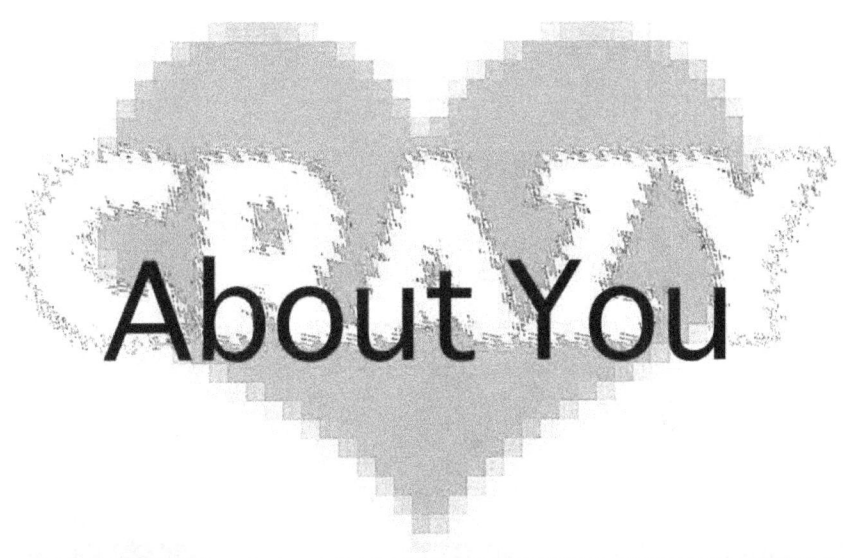

THIS IS MY ART, Part 2
of the darker variety

i know my art is dark & thought-provoking & maybe even scary to certain audiences, & maybe people are thinking, is he okay? is he gonna do himself in tonight? im a little worried; or maybe people are thinking, what an asshole! he just wants to complain, hes only seeking attention, is all———all for a few more LIKEs. but the truth of the matter is, i like this kind of art. when i see art of a darker variety, i feel stimulated, i feel joyful & alive, i feel like im on top of the whole FUCKING world, & i dont know why that is. i like things that bite i guess, for ive always surrounded myself with a more dangerous kind of person, even though to me the average joe was rearing to bite my head off, the prom kings & queens lurking around the corner brandishing switchblades & clubs just waiting for me to come rounding the bend, & you all know what would happen to me then, right? yeah, MY people wear spikes & leather, but YOUR people wear uggs & denim with plastic smiles & phony lives that seem so pathetic but still scare me senseless. you see, i stopped checking out plastic-looking girls one day on the train as i admired these 2 hot preppy-looking girls standing by the door, & then the thought popped in my head: Like fucking a dried-out blow-up doll, your dick chafing the plastic twat in between her legs—painful and gross, right? well, that did it for me; those girls no longer seemed hot anymore & the kind of girls that did intrigue me had piercing scowls carved across their faces, sporting short, spikey hair, with leather jackets dashed & tainted with loads of paint & spikes & studs sticking thru the vacant spaces. thats my kind of girl, this is my kind of art. darkness doesn't seem so scary anymore when youve lived it, like walking thru a haunted house; only the haunted house is your life & the ghouls & goblins hiding in the shadows getting ready to pounce on the first passerby that crosses their paths, are your friends & the only ones left to fear are the quote-unquote normal folk who are wanting to destroy you.

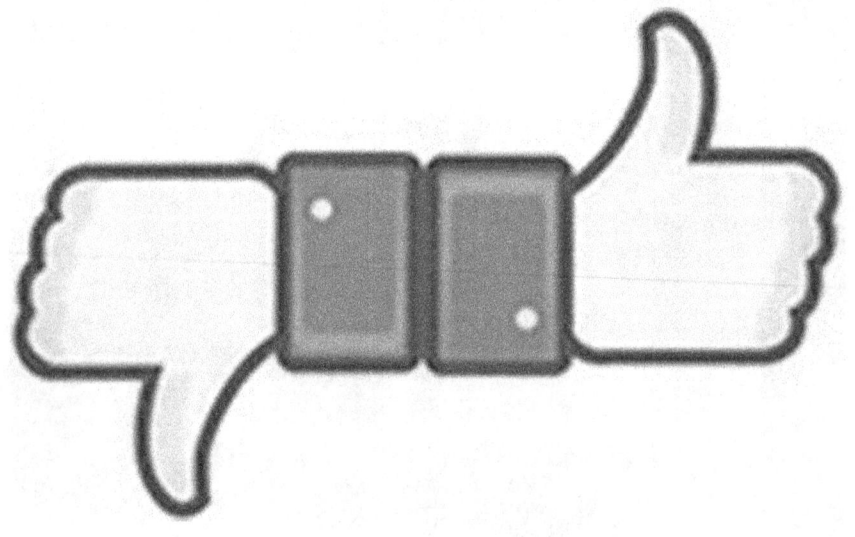

Writing poetry isn't hard. I know a lot of very poetic people who don't even know it themselves. Good poetry comes from the heart, and that's all there is to it. I think the hardest thing about writing poetry is finding the time and having the discipline to do it. And having the balls to call your heart-felt rant a poem.

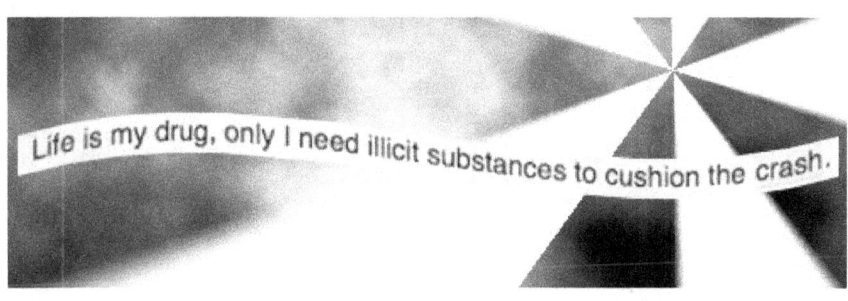

Pogo to Forget

Punk rock has always been my escape from the oppressive 9-to-5 world we live in, my much-needed release that came at the end of every week, where I could see my friends, and a badass band would play and the crowd would go wild. We'd swirl in front of the stage, feet kicking, fists swinging, knees pumping, elbows thrashing. We'd spin. We'd crash and burn, fall to the ground and get lifted up just to be hurled back into the madness. When I was a kid, those were the best times of my life. Taking out all that pent-up aggression in the form of moshing was the greatest thing in the world. Nothing mattered when I was in the pit. Not the girl who rejected me on Monday, the job that fired me on Tuesday, the teacher that failed me on Wednesday, my parents telling me I'm grounded on Thursday, or the big kid that beat me up on Friday — none of it fucking mattered when I was in the pit.

My thoughts are scattered, moving faster than my brain can catch, a haphazard array of a million shooting thoughts, a bouncy ball that just can't be caught. I try and I try, but my ideas are lost. The lines on the page jump like jagged waves. I touch my pen to the line, but it dodges each attempt, so I try and I try, but the lines, so wild and relentless, match the pace of my nervous heart, a pounding so loud, so haphazard—a disaster—that my pulse spikes and my head—yikes! A crazy rhythm—a crazy, crass, spasmodic and fast mess that only I myself made, my thoughts cashing checks that my brain can't catch. An uproarious outterworld in my head, a surreal sort of plane that I dread, über chaos and crude thinking, I can't stop blinking, my lips are tweaking, my vision vile and wild, moving like a shooting star. Because of this, you see—although I don't—my art looks like vomit, so detestable like smeared feces, though in a way it looks great, so remarkably fake. It represents a side of me that I hate. It's almost like standing onstage and farting into the mike, then deemed a genius by fools alike. I guess it would be cruel to say stupidity is a sickness that sticks at birth, a variety of understated answers—none the wiser—and I look for my answers by getting higher. I guess it would be sick to say my brain is cement; my brain is lazy, fat, yet so intelligent. A question about this, and a question about that, a harsh sound sounding so hard in my head; so sharp and fierce, I feel on fire, too many burning desires, too many futile reasons, such pointless force—a hellion of ideas. Sometimes, I must admit—though I'm sorry about this—I feel completely compelled to spray you with the truth. But take my word for it that, the truth coming from me is neurotically sane, though everything I do, it's all unimaginably vain. The human race is corrupt, it's in our nature, it's a disaster of attachments, a fragmented theory, existential proof that at once proves there's a point to all this.

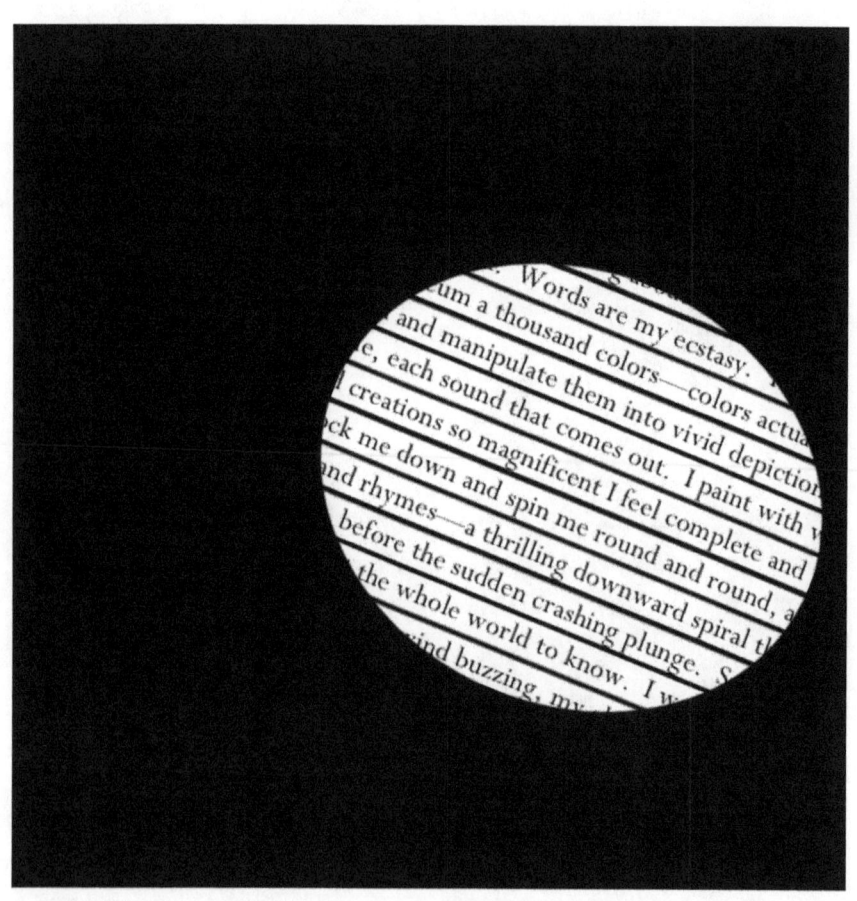

DEAD HITLER

But then the morning comes like a pissed-off landlord collecting the rent.

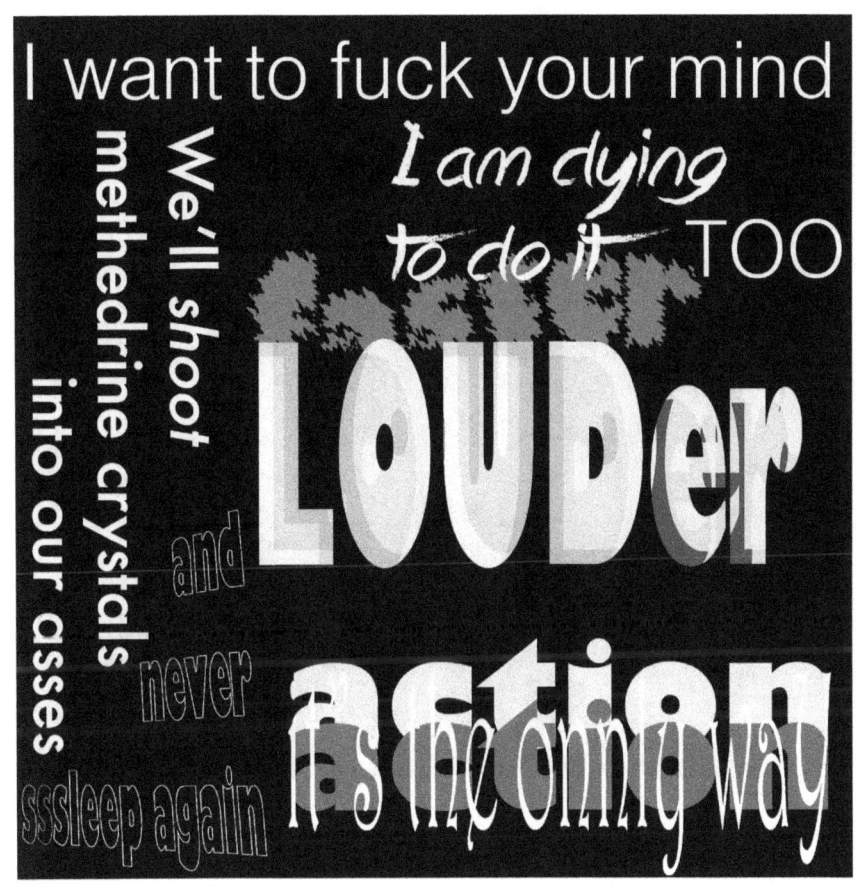

A Shot of Junk

I look through the fog
I stare into yonder as
a shot of junk punches me
in the chest—my heart rebounds
my blood pours through crowded tunnels
like broken subway trains
loaded with cargo, but the cargo speaks
they see hear and dance
my veins shatter as I stumble
through broken lanes of scattered cars
horns blaring and lights zeroing in on
the hole in my head, my brain bubbles and pops//

I'm walking now
walking on air
crawling through clouds of crud
as the shot of junk lifts me up up & up... — ...
I'm falling and flailing as
a blaring ball of hail rips through
my chest cavity
I'm fumbling through day and night
lost in the endless barrage
of broken hearts and twisted bodies
voices like knives
chopping me up and feeding me
to mice, the commotion like
a bubble bath flowing with acid
and crumbling rice
a kick of might in the right spot
on a Friday night, out
out with the crowd
I'm walking on roiling clouds
undulating in spurts of bubbly pus
out in the town—the coppers all
sneer & frown
tumbling down I'm out to lunch
a blundering wet dream creeping through
the streets of death
Where Am I?? I shout
but the demons of lust
the crusty serpents and their dying slaves
of sin and bitterly sucking me
till that shot of junk
licks me again....
A Hit a Puff and a Dying Stab
taking me back to the days of madness
killing my dad with an epic stroke
folding over overdosed and choked
floating away in a puff of smoke

don't get caught in the blistering joke!

Do you ever have those days (nights) when everything you say sounds so poetic and you feel as if it should be featured in a book somewhere? Like your name appearing beside Kerouac in a thick compilation that features the greatest poems ever told. Yeah, well I think I'm having one of those days (nights) right now.

I've got a thought disorder
My thoughts are in disorder

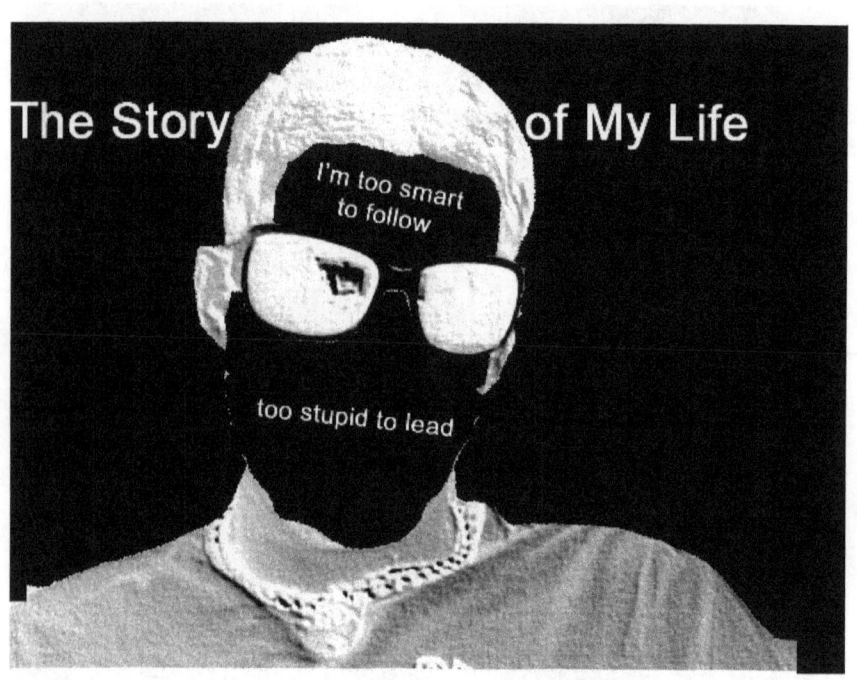

Escape

Why do I do this to
myself?
Deprive myself of the necessities
that one must endure if one wants
to live right
& happy——I'm so unhappy.
Another sleepless night
another racked & aching head.
I stare up at the moon as a shiverous
tremor seizes me, holds me tight.

I'm beating myself raw.
I'm screaming for help, but
nobody can hear me over the
ghouls that stream from my
bloodshot eyes.
I'm seeking pleasure, searching every drawer,
throwing clothes across the floor
knocking books off the shelves,
setting fire to my entire home——the fire

blazes bright & alive....
It ripples & thrashes, & the moon
the dark sky
the stars scattered up there so bright & vivid
make me feel oh so scared & alone.

A waking fit, I'm kicking holes in the ceiling.
I'm throwing plates & bowls
across the kitchen floor
they crunch & crack & scatter
& the sound of breaking & smashing
makes me feel like something
      like something
but I know I'm nothing—tap-tap-tapping my vein.

I lean back & let myself float away
drift upward & the whole world never felt the same.
Why must I
fight reality so often?
You know, reality is kicking my ass all the time.
You know, no I don't, & I thrive on escape
I live for internal mayhem
I need escape, & I'm taking it any way
that I can.

Because it's the only way
out of this place....

Arts & Destruction

Jacked on caffeine, your arms hurtling like nun-chucks, boots coming down in a series of feral stomps, knees pumping as you move like pure fuckin muscle, head shaved clean, replaced with a thin carpet on top, you dart and dash like a madman, thrashing like it's nobody's business but your own—and let it be known!—serious aggression built up from all the repression you experience each and every fuckin day of your life—and now you've come to the Punk rock/Hardcore show to let it all loose on the world.

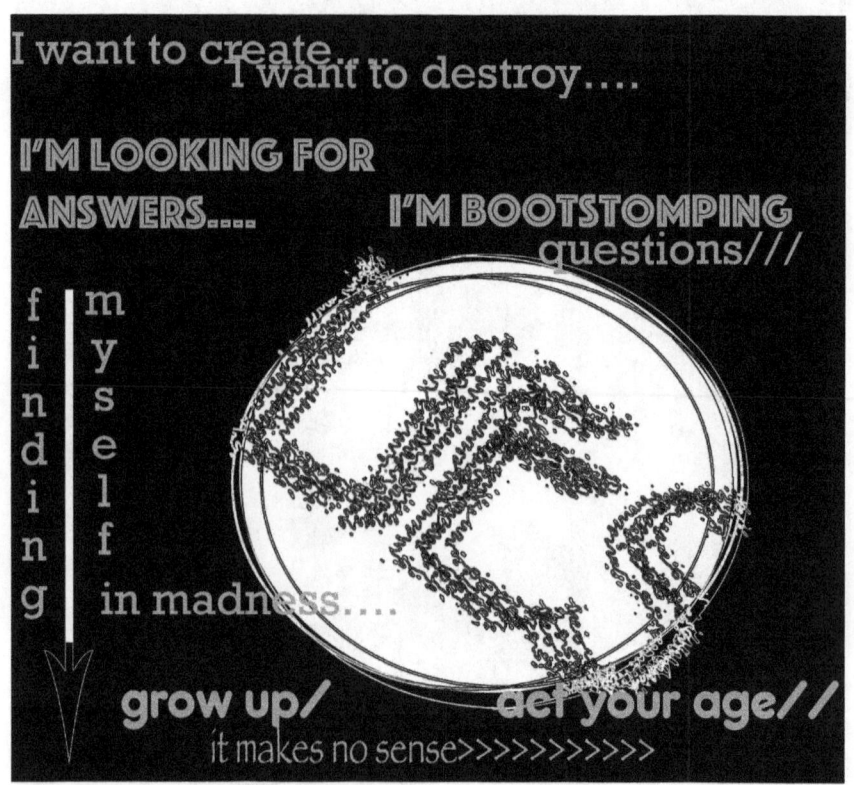

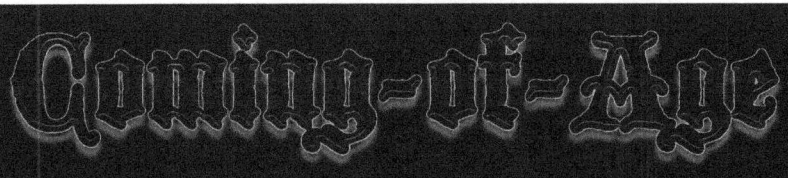

Coming-of-Age

I remember it like it was yesterday, & I wish I didn't—it's just the writer's curse, is all.

Splashing headfirst out of the womb into this thing called reality, which isn't a very fitting title, all things considered. And the doctor looked me square in the eye and said, "Wait a minute, you're not supposed to be here; go back inside"—

—the story of my life....

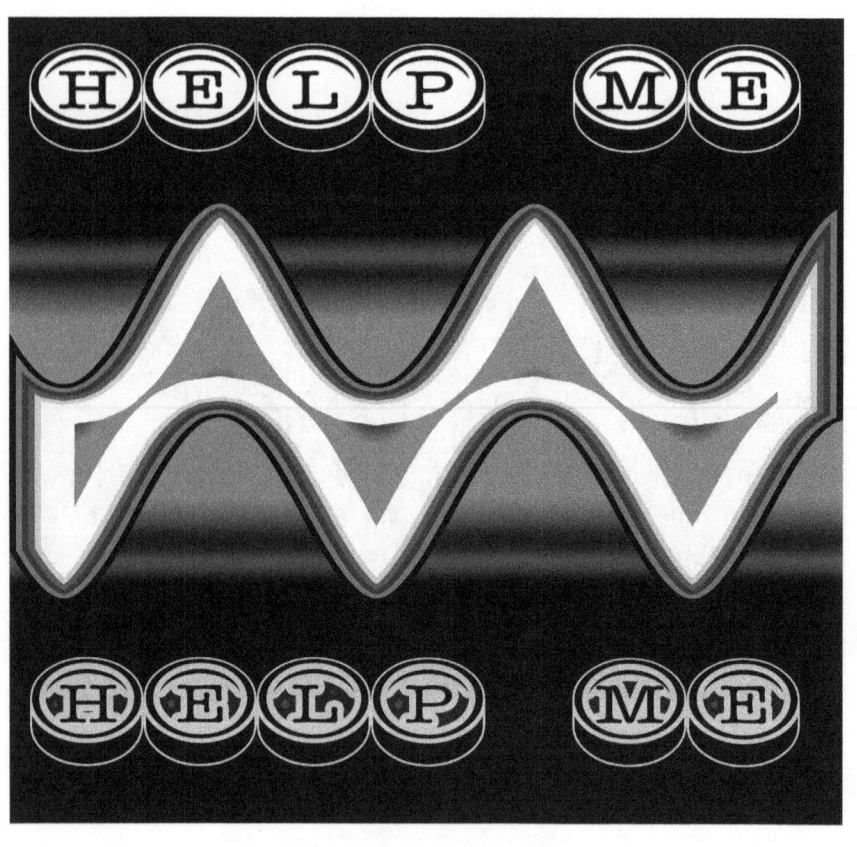

it gibberish that is what we know don't
hammer me know this but it gibberish
got it got it gibberish I'm speaking out
a lensscape of time is the reason i am
here in place first I know you confused
gotta be it inevitable this me pissing on
floor I play mice swimming it no sense
it no sense it gibberish weaving
ribbons around me it gibberish it
gibberish it I don't got you by side it
gibberish please let me run i wanna
run past the firehouse where children
fight and it giberish it giberish help me
as I wonder pointless verses are
nothing but it got me on a string im
tipped upside down cuz it gibberish
because it gibberish becuz it gibberish
what you think shud i end it there pee
pee sperm gism it gibberish

Why the hell am I still awake? I hadn't slept in over 48 hours and all day I've been dragging my body along, just yanking it here and there, my mind blank and blanking out, and yet yet it's 8:09 PM and I'm still pulling myself forward on a tight leash and all afternoon I'd been nodding my head, struggling to keep my eyes open, and yet yet yet it's 8:10 the following night after a no-sleep night.

So why the hell am I still awake?

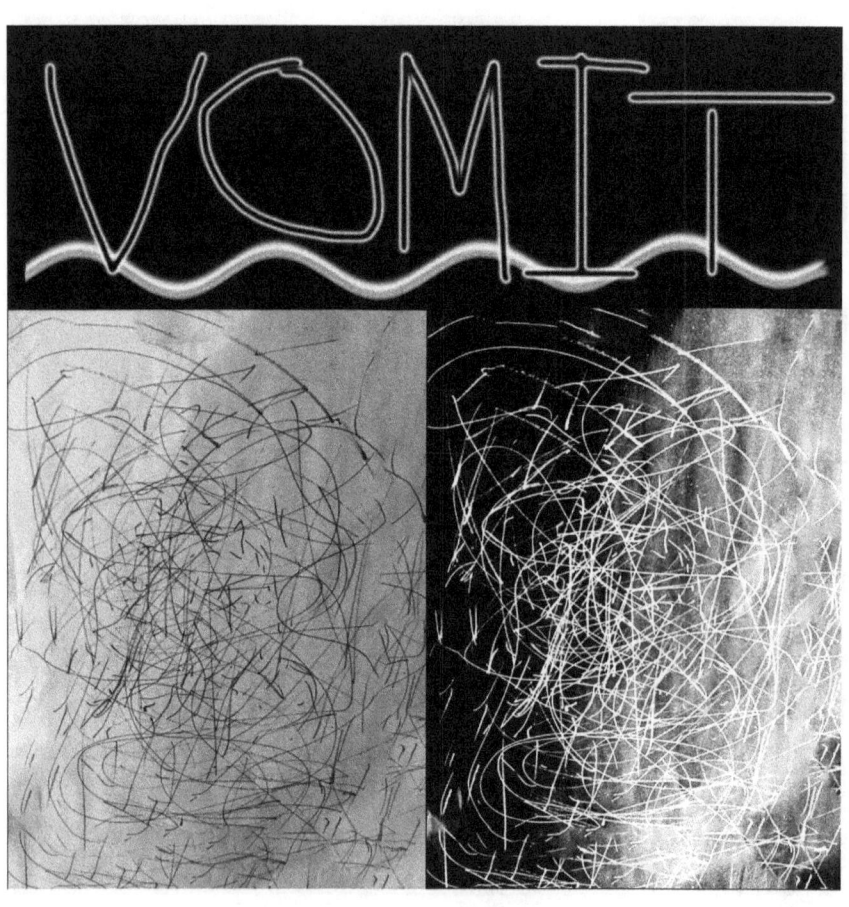

Finger Pointing

I've met many people in my life
different kinds, different breeds,
different colors, different agendas,
different creeds, different religions—
but it's all the same
in the end....

We've all got problems to some extent.
We've all got a reason to hate
being alive.
And I guess that's why I'm not alone.
I guess other people can serve
as a reference point so that
I don't feel like such an ass.

It's hard to coexist without pointing fingers.
It's hard to be a human without
comparing yourself and your circumstances
with other people's lives.
It's hard to live in this world
      so hard
without other people around
because their existence makes my existence
seem not so bad.

There
I said it....

It's been two nights since I slept, just slavering away in my mental prison working on work, unnecessary. You know something's wrong when the cigarettes you smoke, the curling gray exhalation threading its way up to the sky hovering over you like an ecstatic blanket, and the dots, they come to life before your very eyes, dancing and zigzagging across the screen—your depth perception playing relentless games with your hearing and you can hear the music coming from your walls coming from a bush outside, your cat cries in melodic wails that sound an awful lot like the music coming from your walls, and the dots, did I mention the dots? dancing and scattering across the ceiling, and the smoke and the dots and the voices don't sound like my voice anymore, the pitch fluctuating in erratic arrays of turbulence and you want your neighbor to turn off the tunes. You recognize the song now, I bang my fist on the wall and say SHUT IT. The dots and the smoke and then I realize I was the source of the smoke, me, and the dots are still dancing and dancing and dancing and they resemble spiders all coming at me, and I scratch the wall.... I mean I scratch my head, I scratch my balls, I scratch my cat's brain, he stands there and stares at me but I'm not really here, how could I be? In purgatory, maybe, floating suspended above me and there I am typing something about nothing and anything seems to matter when I'm looking into my own head, so detached from reality.

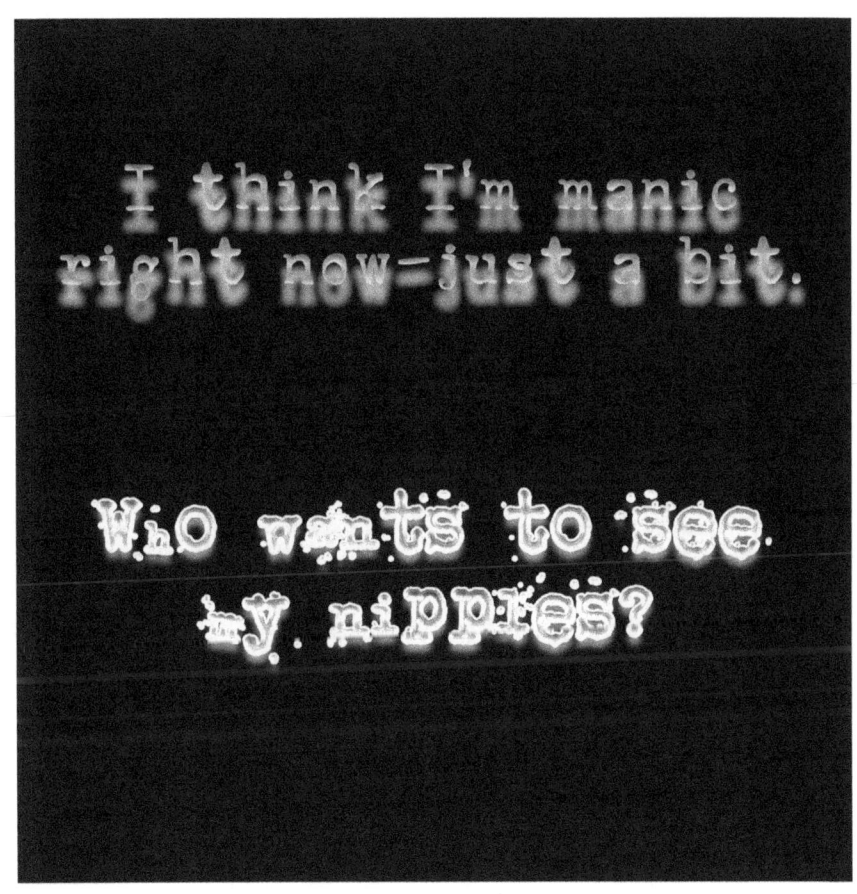

I'm at thrashing Thursday but I'm way too Conceited to Experience a Side of Life that Doesn't exist in my Own head,,,,,, catch my drift? This ain't coexistence, this is MY existence and I'm losing interest in petty problems that don't revolve around me. I will escape the clutches of Time, My Time is Running THIN. Listen LISTEN listen. I'm a disease reaping a twisted breed of Capitalistic horseshit on anyone who chooses to listen as long as I don't HAVE TO listen to you. But listen to this as I solve world hunger, give me a fork and I'll dig on in, give me your money and I'll set it aflame and laugh while watching the news, mediaopolis is a trivial solution to stolen information, so heinous it's like been there done that, right?—steal from the poor and give to the rich, I'm a true grit capitalist, a mutated narcissist seeking salvation in a can of Bud Light, just bash it into my head and howl as loud as I can spit. Fuck the government with a detachable cock that I use as a whiffleball bat in the solitude of my own person circle jerk. It's just how I roll, ya dig?

Sorry, that came out wrong ——— hahaha!

On the Edge of Madness

They Say
Medication Makes Me
Robotic
But I Take Pills Just So
I Can Fall Into
My Brain And See
The World Under A New Lens…
Just So Just So   You Know
Just So I Can Fly Through Space
Talk To Antelopes Who Salute Me
With Crisp Jagged Horns
Become A Cantelope
Drunk By The Rich
Poured Into A Wine Glass
As Great Gusts Of Wind Lift Me
Out Of This Mess I Enter When
The Pants Don't Seem To
Fit Me Quite Right

They Say
Madness
Is No Good
But Is It Madness That Opens
My Eyes   Widens The Mind
Gives Me Wings So I Can Fly
Does It Not Make Me Feel Superb
And 'Crazy'   -A Twisted Sensation
A Jagged Haze That Creates Life
And Murders It Too
I Find I'm Swimming With Sharks
Crawling Through Glaciers Of Shit
Cresting The Putrid Mountainside
And Watching From A Passive Distance
As These 'Normal' People Slaughter Themselves
With Aggro Exchanges And Deadly Stares
Eyes That Project Vomit Through
The Television Set

Is It
Mania
That Makes Me Mad
Or Is It The Torturous Media
A Sleeping Nation Only Awake
To Kill Someone Unsuspecting
And We Give Life To Sleeper Agents
Don't Utter Certain Phrases
Don't Utter Certain Phrases
Or These Agents Of Death Will Hatch From
Distant Places Lurking Only To Murder
Starved Children In The Night
To Murder
Creativity With A Flip Of The Switch
Just Aim And Point
And I Wonder

Is It Me
Or Does Creativity Seem To Be
A Sin In This Day And Age
Like The Creation Of New Thought
Can Cave In Your Head
Like
Thinking Becomes Shunned By
Cool Men In Spartan Uniforms
Waging War On The Persian Army
Like A Repeat Of Thermopylae
It's Retro
So It's Cool, Right
Learn About History So It Doesn't Repeat Itself
Learn About War And Hitler And
Sylvester Stallone
So It Doesn't Happen To Us
Again

Are The 'Sick' So Bad
Is It Not The Good Who Destroy?

I'm Sorry for a Lotta Things
But I'm Not Sorry for Being Me

A BRUTAL MURDER.

Prayers of the Lonely

Lost in midnight's glare, a lonely wolf howls at the solid, glowing moon cuz he's got no one but himself to cherish existence with. What a fright it is to hear the beckoning owl of a stolen dream hoot hoot hoot through the riveting fence that intercepts my connection with nowhere, they beckon me closer toward madness, to my own desertion, dark and derelict; I follow the welcoming call and ignore the many yielding chants of cloaked witches who try to steer me somewhere else, the swirling cauldron of dead children splashing and thrashing—and the owl's stark hooting cuts through the dead of the night, the lonely wolf's bleak howling brings forth a sickening depletion that seems to complete me—my feet rise from the wood chips of fallen hopes and stolen dreams, and I look down as the ground dwindles away like a vaporizing blackhole, and I look up, at the blistering full moon, as the wolf howls and the owl hoots hoots hoots and I'm alone, a deathly brooding seizing me from head to toe and I drift away on the thinnest wisp of smoke like a dastardly wet dream——and I'm alone, lost forever foreboding.

The Rage in My Eyes

The rage in my eyes
burns like a candle left deserted
forgotten tossed to waste,
and you wonder why I hate.

You busy yourself with
magazines that preach peace
and love and all those things.
You avoid me, the way I feel,
looking away so you don't see me

but I see you.

You hide behind a mask.
You live a lie that has seen better days.
You live a life that's sick and filled with vice.
You live in a manner that makes me sick.

~~Nefarious~~ THINGS

Girls   Transitions—

two things that tear me down, all the time, just rip me straight through hell and I don't put up a fight. I welcome the strain that the two forces bring about. I embrace the chaos, the turmoil, some more action drama and disaster. I live for madness. I do my part and they do theirs. We hug and tumble all across my bedroom floor, through my living room, rolling across the kitchen floor and crashing into the oven door, pots and pan clattering out of cabinets and the heated stove catches fire and the whole house burns down. Girls   Transitions, the nefarious things that they are.

Girls, love—it's all too tough for me, but I pull it in and I'm vulnerable against their vicious tug. Like a violent match of tug-of-war, a power struggle that always pulls me in. I'm sliding through the mud as the object of my lust yanks the rope and I'm skittering across dirt and sand and thrown into the blood-red sea. I'm sinking fast and I peek my head out of the redness and see her standing on the shore holding my lifeline—a lifejacket, a fucking lifejacket the only thing that could keep me alive—but she walks away and leaves me to drown.

Transitions, change—fuck me, they got me again. I can't take the unknown as it peers around the edge of the building, watching me as I cut through the alleyway, and then jumps out at me lashing and jams a steak knife through my skull. It's a lethal thing, a terrible vicious beast that holds me in a straightjacket and I'm flailing and thrashing as life fluctuates and laughs, and it's all in flux. Everything's in flux. FLUX. Stop the interchanging the switching courses the coming and going—stop it all before I'm nothing but guts drifting along in the blood-red sea and I see the changes holding hands with the object of my lust and together the two forces walk off into the night.

I'm screaming, can't you see! It's all too much for me.

Gotta Get Outta Here

I'm so tired of the boring crap out there;
so utterly repulsed by the lack of mediums
that people like me have to share our
................art.

Come on, Punks, this is your wakeup call.
This is your chance to produce beautiful crap.
This is your chance to pick through the garbage
and find meaning out of it all.

I say let's go dive into dumpsters;
let's take dirt and make something great.
We'll make something out of nothing
and shove our creations in their fucking faces.

This is our time now, the fuckups of Vermont
banning together to deface all that is pretty.
We have to take a stand against the norm.
We have to stand up to all that is …
<u>boring</u>.

A Turkish Cherry Tree

1.
Life is shit
so let's go and frolic
in the putrid flames of existence.
Dance on
damaged clouds
inhale the toxic fumes
on top of
giant mutated mountains.

2.
I mean
life is really wonderful
when you're looking through
the telescope backwards.
Ain't this such a bashful existence?
I mean
it never is what it is
when you truly think about it

3.
I search for a purpose
another pointless façade
a mask of one thousand faces
just something to pass the time with.

4.
Drift away honey—
go back to yesterday.
We'll scavenge the tainted factories
ramshackle the murderous enchantment of
one million ripe pirates torturing
the cross-eyed love child
of FBI's most wanted knight.

5.
A crash course in vigilante
is what we all really need.
Kill the malevolent leaders
Bring forth a thousand spineless followers
Then shoot the demonic breeders in their heads
and watch as the mutated drones bleed silvery pen ink
down the broken globe's golden spinal column
and
the dead
will
rise again.

It's happened once before
and it'll happened a million times more.

everything i touch turns to shit. and don't say you can relate to this

If it was up to me

I would see to it that everybody on this fucking planet is sodomized and hacked up to pieces.

FUCK EVERYONE
GO TO HELL

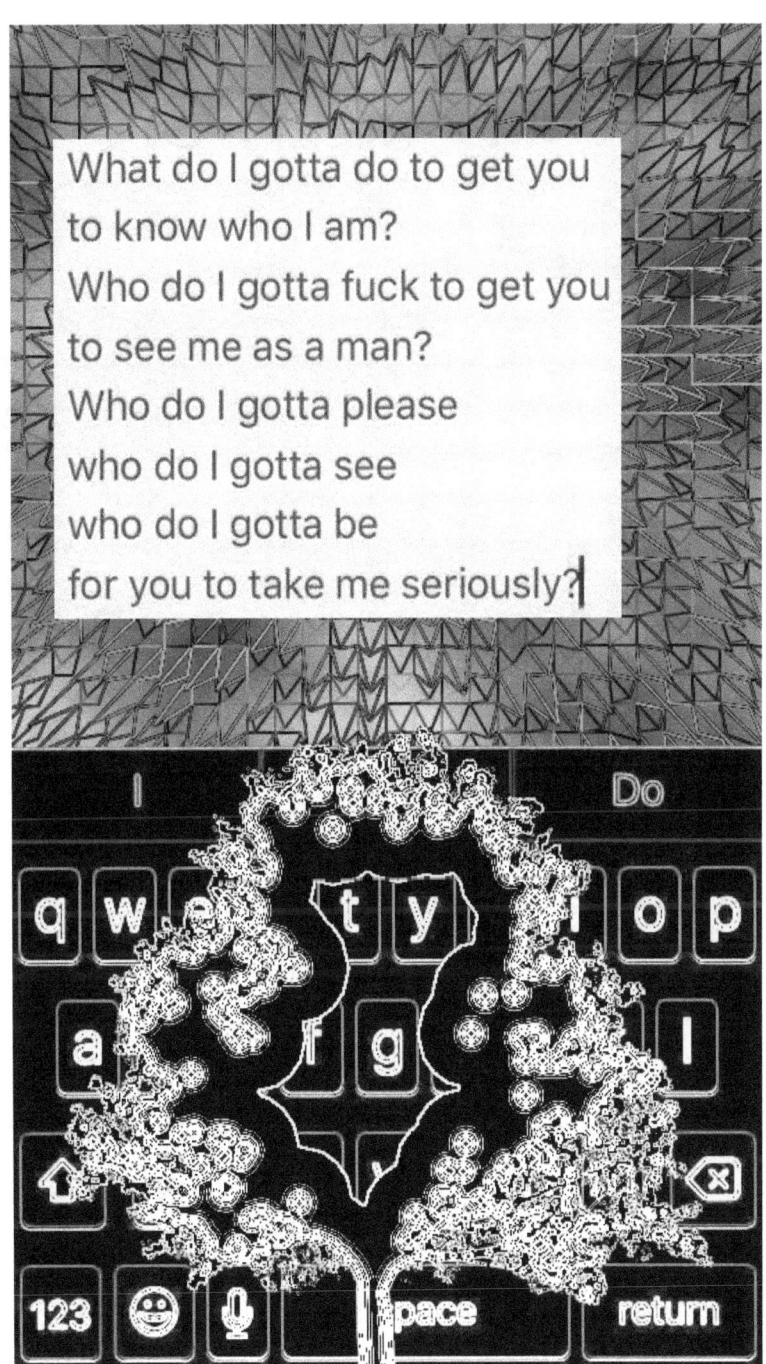

Point & Click

Self-destruct
fuck shit up
    Play it safe
    make no waves
Live on the sly
get real high

too many indecisions
too many lonely opinions
fuck it all
because nothing matters anymore

I'm a hopeless romantic
waiting for something more
than what I'm getting
I'll bathe in chemicals
because nothing matters anymore

Haha, it's all just a joke…..

TOP 5 THINGS
EVERYBODY DOES BUT NOBODY TALKS ABOUT

1. masturbate
2. poop
3. pee
4. vomit

   and

5. justify

"You hate me and I hate you" is almost a universal concept. Why are people too thick to understand that? I can sort of sympathize with them if they can't pick up on the cue right away that somebody dislikes them because, even though to share your dislike, disinterest, distaste, or indifference would be honest, it would be considered rude in this assbackwards society. Society doesn't value the truth; it values the spew of bullshit.

I keep reflecting upon last night as if I had a miraculous revelation. I did, at least to me. In the past, I would fill my emptiness (void) with drugs and alcohol. I would alter my mind in any way possible. I also enjoyed the chaos revolving around round round drugs and alcohol. I was out of control. I was a mess. I didn't give a fuck. I did what I wanted when I wanted to, which is why I got the name Jeremy St. Chaos. Being clean and sober is boring to me. The chaos has dispersed. I am no longer Jeremy St. Chaos. I am empty again. My identity is gone. Without an identity (personality) I am nothing. I am a void. Jeremy Void . . . .
But the chaos came back. I haven't touched a drug or picked up a bottle in about 2 weeks. The quickest way to summarize last night is: After the bar had closed, I told some guy I hadn't had a single drink tonight. He was in shock. I assumed the shock was because I appeared drunk with my natural slur or my care-free swagger. But he said it was because I was having a good time, I was out of control, I was fucking crazy. I didn't drink. I told him I'm just a crazy Punk rocker. It was miraculous. I was Jeremy St. Chaos again, but sober. I'm back. . . . The void has not yet been filled but I'm working on it. At least I got my identity back, if even for just one night . . . .

Terrorism: To induce terror in our hearts and souls; Victory: To maintain a state of constant terror; Defeat: To let the terror in to fester and rot; Freedom: To be rid of bondage and outside influence. Rights: the right to be safe.

The terrorists have won, we run scared every day of our lives, through security checkpoints and body scans at the airport, through fields of candid cameras peeping on us you just can't get away.
We're stuck in a terminal state of fear, we're lost hoping they don't get us here, ISIS, Al Quaeda, the big bad Taliban lurking around every corner, can't take a shower without fear that the walls will erupt without fear that stepping out of the shower means meeting a barrage of bullets as they splice through the walls and sever your heart from your soul.
There's nowhere to turn nowhere to run, because everywhere you go Osama's henchmen are locked and loaded, the schools are not safe, run away, for fear of what might be around the bend waiting to chop you down.
Terrorism: to evoke fear.
Terrorism: to control us with acts of terror....
It's sad and I'm scared of the worldly toughguys wielding explosive swords, pens that nuke bridges, clip on ties that if you were to yank on them airplanes would come railing through the sky and colliding with your child's school.
Run away before they win.
Run away admit defeat before the fuckers win.
Protect the women & children protect ourselves.
Death is inevitable but please oh please don't bring us there....
We're in a state of fear but there are worse things to fear than pussy gunmen who hide in shadows trained assassins who wait for the precise moment to pull and next thing gunfire punches holes in everything in sight, there's worse things to fear than that
like the United States Government, for one.
Like the police marching like Gestapo withdrawing guns and firing them at innocents people
 beating kids up in the street/
But it's funny isn't it? if we're scared of them then we ain't got a single fight left in us, like look at a boxer who's too scared to enter the ring, just waiting for that knockout punk to come jarring into his jaw bone and out go his lights as he drops to the mat with a heavy clack, see that's all that fear does, it keeps us weak and passive and terrorists can go home feeling gratified at a job well done at a country stuttering and afraid....

That's all that it does///

●●●●○ Verizon LTE 4:16 PM ✱ 🔋

Cancel   **Update Status**   Post

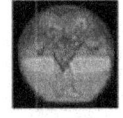 Jeremy Void
🌐 Public ▼

What's on your mind?

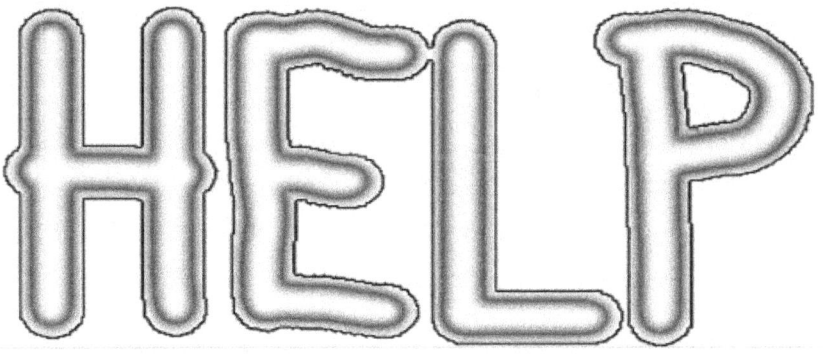

I don't really care how others perceive Punk. Not good, I'd assume. But each one of those assholes looking down on Punks are probably at home shooting dope and smoking crack and drinking themselves to death while we're out drinking to live, fighting for kicks, and living it up. Fuck those boring cunts. They mean as much to me as the scum beneath my shoes and the plaque on my teeth.

A block of time of space, a place to transcribe word after word in a roiling mass of cloudy oblivion. This is what I'm going to do, going to try doing, try to do. I'm going to create a solid fusion of word vomit wrapped between two slices of bread and served with a lovely basket of fries on the side. Where do I start? I was thinking about being a kid and I used to vomit all down the side of the street. I'd just be walking along, feel it coming up, duck, and pitch it onto the street, spray it outward for the whole world to see. I had a friend and I was walking with him and my first girlfriend was there too and she cringed and said yuk as she stammered backwards, and this friend of mine just said no no no that's just Jeremy he vomits. He vomits all the time. You'll get used to it. Iggy Pop vomited onstage and that was cool right? Everybody laughed and thought it funny, egged him on, screaming encore encore! But that's Iggy Pop, he can get away with walking on the stage like a runway model, walking on and then it all comes up and what's he gonna do about it? He's stuck there because his band is playing and in fact he is his band, he himself is his entire band because of the name he carries around, Iggy Pop, so what's he to do? Vomit spew puke barf, whatever you wanna call it, it all came up in a dashing and disgusting waterfall spilling out from his jowls. Johnny Rotten spits. Iggy Pop vomits. GG Allin eats his own shit and forces chicks to suck his dick while onstage. What an asshole he was, and yet everybody loved him. What a disgrace he was too. All he wanted was to be hated, and yet in response he built up a huge fanbase of loving Punk rockers who would love nothing more but to let him put it up their asses. Bunch of queers, if you ask me. But then, didn't I say I'd let Richard Hell give it to me? I think I said that on film and the video is currently on YouTube available for the whole world to see, to see me make a fool of myself, a drunken mockery was me. Okay, now, I felt like I was cool back then, and years ago I would have watched that video and laughed at the foolishness that was once me, that was Jeremy St. Chaos, Darby Crash incarnate, a king in his own mind who actually truly honest-to-God said his shit smells like flowers. It doesn't smell like shit it smells like flowers, he wrote in an email in response to his best friend claiming that he'd been acting like his shit don't stink for the past few days weeks and months, maybe even a year I don't know. So he moved to Vermont and changed his name to Jeremy Void, that doesn't mean he's a new person living in a brand-new era, a brand-new age, it doesn't mean shit, except that this Jeremy you speak of is a hackjob, a phony, so full of himself he's rearing to explode, balls of cum and spit and snot and _vomit_ nonetheless come spraying up and out and splashing in his fans' faces. A guy's gotta dream right? I have big dreams low expectations when my expectations used to be skyrocketing through the roof, and nobody lived up to them nobody even tried because I was just not important enough for that ever for someone to try and impress me to try and make me happy. No I was not that special. I was a loser everyone knew it too. But I feel like I've changed or maybe that's my ego talking, my out-of-proportion undeserving-of arrogance that sometimes springs out and slaps my fellow man in the face and my fellow woman in the butt just rubs their tits and sneers through dirty teeth as they smile and scowl all at once not really sure how to feel about all this. I mean why is this strange man doing that to me they might be thinking. Because I can, is what I'm thinking back, only don't you think it's strange that I know what the molested women are thinking, maybe in a perfect world I would. In a perfect world I would know what everyone is thinking, especially what you are thinking you the reader, because if I knew that I'd know how to get your attention, lasso it with a trail of barbed-wire, spikes ripping into your neck as I yank the cord and you surge out of your seat leaving a bloody trail behind shaped like your dragged and beaten body being pulled up and down the dirt road, this way and that back and forth, the whole nine yards, yadda yadda, as the retards who don't know English would say—yadda yadda, blah blah blah, etc. etc. I guess I say blah blah blah a lot and I will end it that way—blah blah blah.

but in the end i hate YOU so much more than i hate me because in the end you made me who i am and i will make you fuckin pay; but then again, what does it matter anyway? because we all suck, we're all shit, the world is burning down around us, and I will see to it that it continues burning until there's nothing left but ashes

What Happened to Those Days??

Samantha, i love you, even though i'll probly never hear from you again.

Andrew, i miss you, we were blood brothers, who the fuck is gonna travel the country with me like we've been talkin bout for a while now, or more importantly who the fuck is gonna play guitar for lethal erection when i get back.

And all the adventures, like Russel, at fuckin store 24 the asshole tryin to look tough in front of his girl, or when we were with lacey at the fountain in copley spangin & i went into the packie every 20 minutes to get 40s so that after the 4th time goin in they just stopped sellin em to us, and wen i got that high school cunt to buy us all mad dog & give Kyle (since he don't drink) $10.

And bell, i miss gettin drunk at ur place & the BBQs, or gettin drunk at Deenas place and i always managed to get somebody pst at me, or sittin in ur bathtub while a chicken was sittin and shittin on my head, & 4th of July when i threw the fuckin smoke grenade at the gees, & when i backed up into the car parked across the street from Chunkys house after the show at the ICC church where i fell through the window & that cunt, hardcore kid, security guard (who i wudn't wanna fuck with) almost caught us for tryin to steal the PA from the church then later the packie thought we were tryin to rob him so pulled out a baseball bat from the counter. I still remember when u started yellin at the spic mbta janitor to show you his green card cuz he got mad cuz u were pukin at the train station.

And Derrick, the fuckin hippie show we wrecked (Andrew was there too). Singin 'Nervous Breakdown' for ADHD (Now known as TKO Disorder), or singin 'Lexicon Devil' for the Welfare Brats.

And Ryan, I still remember when i was 21 and you were 19 and u passed out outside of a bar so i cracked a beer open and put it beside ur head then went in the bar and someone called the cops cuz they saw me give u the beer. Or fuckin anime night when u convinced me that hot girl was really a guy so i asked her which turned out you already knew it was a girl and thought she was hot but u just wanted me to go ask her. Or when everyone ditched me cuz the cops were commin and i was too wasted to walk, u were the only one who stayed back with me.

And DP, i dunno what fuckin happened to u, but we used to have a lotta fun then u disappeared, but i miss you too.

Don't mean to be all sentimental and shit but i can't help it. i miss those fuckin days. Now times are changin and everyone and everything is movin forward and i'm bein left behind. Things change, but i'd imagine that i'd change with them. And again, i was wrong. I miss Boston & i miss all my friends.

I look to the sky
at times of distress.
The rainbow blossoms
like a bloody carcass.
Butterflies bloom, careening
like vampire bats dive-bombing
and scooping up rats.
It's a glorious day when
the sun melts like candle wax,
and flowers spit acid into
the eyes of stray cats, who
fight each other like mountain lions.

I have this theory that when people see my name associated with anything, they look away and simply ignore it. Which might just be my low self-esteem talking; I don't know. I've just kind of been feeling really depressed these past few days. I've been a nobody my entire life, and I'm just sick of being ignored all the time. When I was in Boston and using heavily, people couldn't ignore me because I was really aggressive and intense, and I pissed off so many people in the process, which is what I wanted to begin with. But I didn't want this. I always dreamed of being infamous, because I thought the only way to get a name for myself was by doing something bad, by being bad. But I've finally taken that aggression and turned it into something positive, and people probably just think, Oh, that's just Jeremy, he's up to his same old tricks. But I'm not angry all the time, that's the thing. I'm not breaking shit anymore. I'm not destroying myself or anyone else. I'm not stealing, lying, or cheating. I'm not doing anything I used to do, because I've started anew. But the thing is, I still have that drive to be antisocial, and I guess that's why my writing is so important to me; it gives me a positive means to be, as someone put it the other day, that "same angry nihilist Punk" I once was.

Am I

- ⓐ an artist
- ⓑ a crass technician
- ⓒ a lewd bazooka
- ⓔ a crazy mad scientist
- ⓕ an insomniac battling fantastic demons that come crawling out of my dresser drawer when I least expect it, with razor-sharp eyeballs
- ⓖ or all of the above

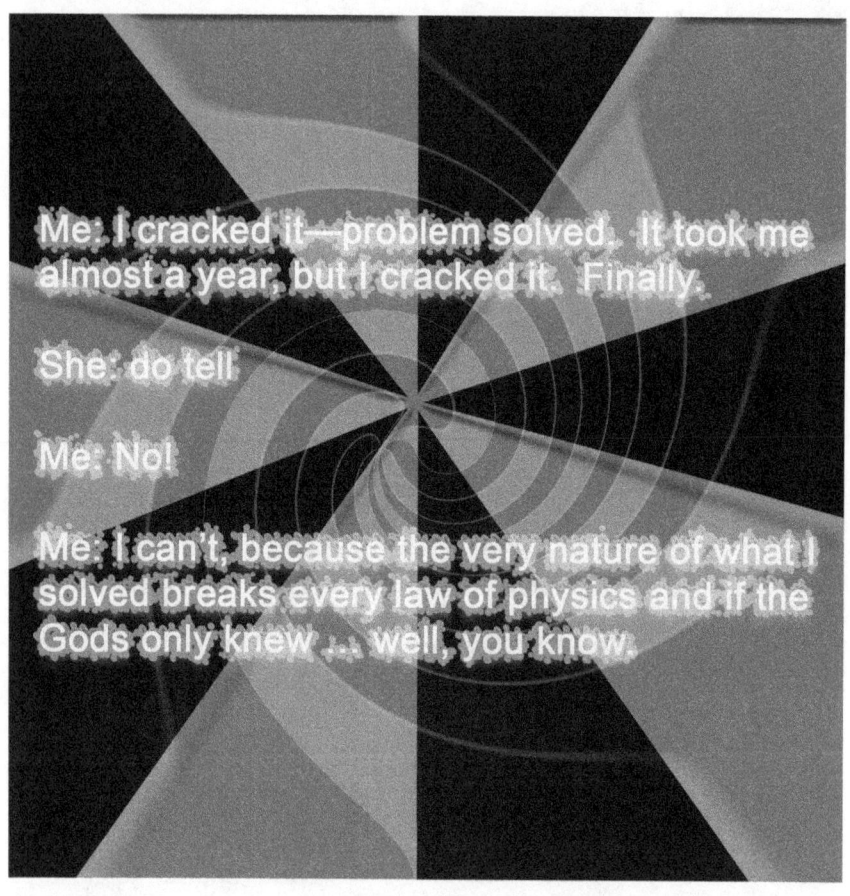

Me: I cracked it—problem solved. It took me almost a year, but I cracked it. Finally.

She: do tell

Me: No!

Me: I can't, because the very nature of what I solved breaks every law of physics and if the Gods only knew ... well, you know.

Credit Where Credit's Due

intro (Pp. vii)
>This is my information on Facebook.

WANTED (Pp. 3)
>This was originally a newspaper clipping I had found on Yahoo Images. The pictures are my actual mugshots from when I had been arrested for possession of cocaine at the age of 19.

29 (Pp. 5)
>Hunter S. Thompson is a well-renounced author.

Punk Rock (Pp. 10)
>999, the Clash, the Adverts, Cock Sparrer, and the Adicts are all Punk rock bands from the late '70s.

WHO ARE THESE PUNKS? (Pp. 12)
>These were originally a newspaper clipping I had found on Yahoo Images. The picture in the middle is of me at a Lethal Erection band practice years ago. The thumbs-down is the LIKE symbol on Facebook.

Point & Click (Pp. 15)
>I took this picture in Montreal, Canada.

Punks Not Dead (Pp. 17)
>This saying dates back to the early '80s.

What's on your mind? (Pp. 18)
>This is a screenshot of the status box on Facebook, on my computer.

A STRANGE MURDER CASE (Pp. 19)
>This was originally a newspaper clipping I had found on Yahoo Images.

Punk Rock Hits Town (Pp. 31)
>This was originally a newspaper clipping I had found on Yahoo Images.

Punk Rock Song (Pp. 35)
>In this picture is Lethal Erection playing at the Knights of Columbus in Newton, MA.

SMILE (Pp. 42)
> I took the picture on top in downtown Rutland, VT.

Arts & Destruction (Pp. 47)
> This was originally a newspaper clipping I had found on Yahoo Images.

death (Pp. 51)
> This is a screenshot of the search box on Facebook.

cruising (Pp. 53)
> The Lower Class Brats are a Punk rock band.

DAILY NEWS (Pp. 56)
> This was originally a newspaper clipping I had found on Yahoo Images.

Point & Click (Pp. 61)
> I took this picture in Montreal, Canada.

DEATH TO FASCIST PUNKS (Pp. 64)
> "Punk Rock Community" is a group on Facebook.

Decisions (Pp. 71)
> This is a screenshot of the different reactions on Facebook.

Getting Hands Wet (Pp. 92)
> This was originally a newspaper clipping I had found on Yahoo Images.

PUNKS KILL DRUG STAR (Pp. 101)
> This was originally a newspaper clipping I had found on Yahoo Images

No / Yes (Pp. 102)
> I found this picture on Yahoo Images.

Obituaries (Pp. 103)
> This was originally a newspaper clipping I had found on Yahoo Images.

Point & Click (Pp. 109)
> I took this picture in Montreal, Canada.

Everybody is Somebody (Pp. 112)
> This was originally a newspaper clipping I had found on Yahoo Images.

Chicago Sun-Times (Pp. 117)
> This was originally a newspaper clipping I had found on Yahoo Images.

frenzy (Pp. 122)
> This was originally a newspaper clipping I had found on Yahoo Images.

Who's the Fag? by Lethal Erection (Pp. 123)
> This is a song sung by my old band Lethal Erection, from our album *Fucked by the Law.*

time killer (Pp. 128)
> This was originally a newspaper clipping I had found on Yahoo Images

DAILY NEWS (Pp. 134)
> This was originally a newspaper clipping I had found on Yahoo Images.

Kill Rats (Pp. 137)
> This was originally a newspaper clipping I had found on Yahoo Images.

Give a Book, Take a Book (Pp. 143)
> I took this picture in the Ace & Bloomer building, which is the building that houses all the government offices in Rutland, VT.

THE DEAD WALK (Pp. 145)
> This was originally a newspaper clipping I had found on Yahoo Images.

News Head (Pp. 150)
> This was originally a newspaper clipping I had found on Yahoo Images.

Another Piece of the Puzzle, Obtained (Pp. 151)
> In this picture is me and an old friend.

Daily Mirror (Pp. 152)
> This was originally a newspaper clipping I had found on Yahoo Images.

Arts & Entertainment (Pp. 160)
> This was originally a newspaper clipping I had found on Yahoo Images.

Point & Click (Pp. 161)
> I took this picture in Montreal, Canada.

World (Pp. 166)
> This was originally a newspaper clipping I had found on Yahoo Images.

Obsession (Pp. 176)
> This was originally a magazine article I had found on Yahoo Images. The picture on the bottom is of me.

Anti-Fashion Week (Pp. 178)
    This was originally a magazine article I had found on Yahoo Images.

MORE DEVELOPEMENTS (Pp. 182)
    This was originally a newspaper clipping I had found on Yahoo Images.

Kids on the flip side of life (Pp. 190)
    This was originally a newspaper clipping I had found on Yahoo Images.

No Respect (Pp. 196)
    Pub 42 is a bar in downtown Rutland, VT.

Hard Times (Pp. 202)
    In this picture is me and an old girlfriend.

KILLER BEHIND SOMEONE'S DOOR? (Pp. 203)
    This was originally a newspaper clipping I had found on Yahoo Images.

News Clipping (Pp. 208)
    This was originally a newspaper clipping I had found on Yahoo Images.

Fuck the Chaffee (Pp. 213)
    The Chaffee Art Center is the main art museum in Rutland, VT.

Point & Click (Pp. 223)
    I took this picture in Montreal, Canada.

humdrum, boring people (Pp. 228)
    This was originally a newspaper clipping I had found on Yahoo Images.

Too late (Pp. 230)
    This was originally a newspaper clipping I had found on Yahoo Images.

Arts & Destruction (Pp. 234)
    This was originally a newspaper clipping I had found on Yahoo Images.

Lack of bodies doesn't prove there's no serial killer (Pp. 236)
    This was originally a newspaper clipping I had found on Yahoo Images.

Hipsters "R" Us (Pp. 239)
    "Oi, oi, skinheads. Get your own club" is an old Punk rock saying.

U.S. DECLARES WAR (Pp. 254)
    This was originally a newspaper clipping I had found on Yahoo Images.

Commemorating 50 years in 50 hours (Pp. 256)
: This was originally a newspaper clipping I had found on Yahoo Images.

someday everyone is going to hate me (Pp. 270)
: In the background holding the flip phone is the current drummer of Lethal Erection Pat's twin brother.

Point & Click (Pp. 278)
: I took this picture in Montreal, Canada.

Ill-fated (Pp. 282)
: This was originally a newspaper clipping I had found on Yahoo Images.

A Guy who is all smiles (Pp. 284)
: This was originally a newspaper clipping I had found on Yahoo Images.

We are friends, right? (Pp. 290)
: This is a screenshot of the comment box on Facebook, on my computer.

Page 9 (Pp. 292)
: This was originally a newspaper clipping I had found on Yahoo Images.

Forgotten heroes (Pp. 295)
: This was originally a newspaper clipping I had found on Yahoo Images.

Broken LIKE (Pp. 302)
: This is a screenshot of the LIKE button Facebook.

SETTING IT STRAIGHT (Pp. 305)
: This was originally a newspaper clipping I had found on Yahoo Images.

The Three Stooges Plus 1 (Pp. 322)
: This was originally a newspaper clipping I had found on Yahoo Images.

No killer doing time (Pp. 324)
: This was originally a newspaper clipping I had found on Yahoo Images.

Point & Click (Pp. 325)
: I took this picture in Montreal, Canada.

Racing Thoughts (Pp. 326)
: Pikachu is a character from Pokemon, which is something I absolutely despise, I must add.

BULLIED TO DEATH (Pp. 330)
>   This was originally a newspaper clipping I had found on Yahoo Images.

Peace Returns (Pp. 333)
>   This was originally a newspaper clipping I had found on Yahoo Images.

Porn Film Actress Stoned to Death (Pp. 348)
>   This was originally a newspaper clipping I had found on Yahoo Images.

Point & Click (Pp. 361)
>   I took this picture in Montreal, Canada.

DAILY NEWS (Pp. 362)
>   This was originally a newspaper clipping I had found on Yahoo Images.

The Art World (Pp. 377)
>   www.bandcamp.com is an independent record label online.

WHITE RIOT (Pp. 386)
>   This was originally a newspaper clipping I had found on Yahoo Images.

Youth thugs in savage attack on shop owner (Pp. 389)
>   This was originally a newspaper clipping I had found on Yahoo Images.

Decisions (Pp. 390)
>   This is a screenshot of the LIKE button Facebook.

DEAD HITLER (Pp. 399)
>   This was originally a newspaper clipping I had found on Yahoo Images.

Arts & Destruction (Pp. 408)
>   This was originally a newspaper clipping I had found on Yahoo Images.

Fuckin Aggro to the Max! (Pp. 409)
>   This is a picture of the moshpit from when the Business, which is a Punk rock band from the early '80s, played at Club Lido, in Revere, MA.

Thrashing Thursdays (Pp. 420)
>   Thrashing Thursdays is a thrash/metal show on Thursday at the Local, which is a bar in downtown Rutland, VT.

A Brutal Murder (Pp. 423)
>   This was originally a newspaper clipping I had found on Yahoo Images.

A STRANGE MURDER CASE (Pp. 426)
> This was originally a newspaper clipping I had found on Yahoo Images.

Point & Click (Pp. 432)
> I took this picture in Montreal, Canada.

Daily News (Pp. 433)
> This was originally a newspaper clipping I had found on Yahoo Images.

Punk Rock Hits Town (Pp. 434)
> This was originally a newspaper clipping I had found on Yahoo Images.

What's on your mind? (Pp. 441)
> This is a screenshot of the status box on Facebook, on my iPhone.

Vogue (Pp. 442)
> This was originally the front cover of a magazine I had found on Yahoo Images.

Word Vomit (Pp. 444)
> Richard Hell, GG Allin, Richard Hell, and Johnny Rotten are all Punk musicians from the '70s.

www.ingramcontent.com/pod-product-compliance
Lightning Source LLC
Chambersburg PA
CBHW020728160426
43192CB00006B/147